What People Like You Are Saying about *Heaven's Song*:

"Not only is this West's best work to date, but it is essential for anyone ready for the 'next step' in their study of the Theology of the Body. You shouldn't read this book casually for head-knowledge, but with the heart and on the knees!"

— *Damon O, West Orange, NJ*

"*Heaven's Song* dug down into my heart and brought out a deeper and more pure love for my husband and for God. It is truly amazing!"

— *Dana V, West Chester, PA*

"The words of Christopher West have changed my heart and view of my femininity in a profound and holy way. Please read this book! Your life will never be the same because you will meet Jesus in a most intimate way!"

— *Julie W, New York, NY*

"This book sings! And in singing it teaches us to sing. With Christopher West's help in pulling back the veil on the profound mystery of God's spousal love, we discover that the lyrics and the melody of 'heaven's song' have been in our hearts all along!"

— *Bill D, Lansdowne, PA*

"The deeper I got into this book, the more in awe I was of God's stunning plan for us. I've been a Catholic my whole life — why hasn't anybody told me this!? I challenge all men to read *Heaven's Song*. Guys, trust me, you'll see, like I did, that sexual love is more amazing and sacred then we ever dreamed!"

— *Steve M, Tampa, FL*

"*Heaven's Song* shines the light of Christ on our wounds only to be drawn into the healing balm of his Glory. We woman get in trouble when fear sets in. This book encourages us to turn our hearts to the Father's love, to press in, to receive and to be not afraid."

— *Nicole R, Melbourne, FL*

"Transforming union with Jesus is a fruit of a mature and integrated sexual identity. This is the call given through *Heaven's Song* and it is my prayer that many priests, religious, and laity alike will read this book and respond to the call."

— *Father Jim, Sellersville, PA*

"Christopher West has done an outstanding job in *Heaven's Song* of showing us how passionately God loves us. I felt as if I were right within the heartbeat of God's mercy and love."

— *Matt D, Denver, CO*

Heaven's Song

Heaven's Song

Sexual Love as it was Meant to Be

BASED ON THE HIDDEN TALKS OF JOHN PAUL II'S THEOLOGY OF THE BODY

Christopher West

Foreword by Most Reverend Robert J. Carlson,
Bishop of Saginaw

ASCENSION PRESS

West Chester, Pennsylvania

Ascension Press
Post Office Box 1990
West Chester, PA 19380
Orders: 1-800-376-0520
www.AscensionPress.com

Cover design: Devin Schadt

Printed in the United States of America
08 09 10 11 7 6 5 4 3 2 1

ISBN: 978-1-934217-46-7

To the gate of heaven,
the all beautiful one,
Mary.

Also by Christopher West

Good News About Sex and Marriage: Answers to Your Questions about Catholic Teaching (Servant, 2000; revised edition, 2006)

Theology of the Body Explained: A Commentary on John Paul II's Man and Woman He Created Them (Pauline, 2003; revised edition, 2007)

Theology of the Body for Beginners: A Basic Introduction to John Paul II's Sexual Revolution (Ascension, 2004; revised edition, 2008)

The Love That Satisfies: Reflections on Eros and Agape (Ascension, 2007)

Contents

Abbreviations

CCC   *Catechism of the Catholic Church*, second edition (Libreria Editrice Vaticana, 1997)

CL   *Cantata of Love: A Verse by Verse Reading of the Song of Songs*, by Blaise Arminjon (Ignatius Press, 1988)

CTH   *Crossing the Threshold of Hope*, John Paul II (Knopf, 1994)

CW   *The Collected Works of Saint John of the Cross* (ICS Publications, 1991)

DC   *Deus Caritas Est*, Pope Benedict XVI's Encyclical Letter *God is Love* (Pauline, 2006)

EA   *Ecclesia in America*, John Paul II's Apostolic Exhortation on the Church in America (Pauline, 1999)

FC   *Familiaris Consortio*, John Paul II's Apostolic Exhortation on the Christian Family (Pauline, 1981)

FS   *Through the Year with Bishop Fulton Sheen*, Henry Dieterich (Ignatius Press, 2003)

GM   *Gift and Mystery*, John Paul II's reflections on the fiftieth anniversary of his priestly ordination (Doubleday, 1996)

GS   *Gaudium et Spes*, Vatican II's Pastoral Constitution on the Church in the Modern World (Pauline, 1965)

LF   *Letter to Families*, John Paul II's Letter in the Year of the Family (Pauline, 1994)

LR   *Love and Responsibility*, Karol Wojtyla's philosophical work on sexuality (Ignatius Press, 1993)

MCS   *Mary: The Church at the Source*, Joseph Cardinal Ratzinger and Hans Urs Von Balthasar (Ignatius Press, 2005)

MD   *Mulieris Dignitatem*, John Paul II's Apostolic Letter on the Dignity and Vocation of Women (Pauline, 1988)

MI   *Memory and Identity*, John Paul II's final memoir (Rizzoli, 2005)

MTB   *The Virgin Mary and Theology of the Body*, Donald H. Calloway, editor (Marian Press, 2005)

NMI   *Novo Millennio Ineunte*, John Paul II's Apostolic Letter at the Close of the Jubilee Year (Pauline, 2001)

SL   *The Spirit of the Liturgy*, Joseph Cardinal Ratzinger (Ignatius, 2000)

SM   *The Secret of Mary*, St. Louis de Montfort, adapted by Eddie Doherty (Montfort Publications, 1998)

SSV   *Sex and Sacredness: A Catholic Homage to Venus*, Christopher Derrick (Ignatius Press, 1982)

SS   *Spe Salvi*, Pope Benedict XVI's Encyclical Letter *Saved in Hope* (Pauline, 2007)

TD   *True Devotion to the Blessed Virgin*, St. Louis de Montfort (Montfort Publications, 1993)

TOB   *Man and Woman He Created Them: A Theology of the Body*, John Paul II's general audience addresses on Human Love in the Divine Plan (Pauline, 2006)

VS   *Veritatis Splendor*, John Paul II's Encyclical Letter on the Splendor of Truth (Pauline, 1993)

Acknowledgments

I am grateful to the following men and women who have helped me with this book:

Bishop Robert Carlson, Ed Hogan, Lorraine Ranalli, Nicole Rodriguez, Fr. John Horn, Fr. Jim Otto, Matthew Dalton, Damon Owens, Bill Donaghy, Maureen Snook, Dana Vink, Michael J. Miller, Matthew Pinto, Steve Motyl, Christopher Cope, John Harden, Michael Flickinger, Michael Fontecchio, and Wendy West.

Foreword

A good priest and spiritual director I know sometimes asks
people, "What song is God singing over you today?"

In this book on the undelivered addresses of John Paul II's Theology
of the Body, Christopher West invites us to open our ears to the song
that God is singing to us through our bodies, through our creation as
male and female, and through our natural desire for intimate union.
The invitation to hear this song – which tells us of God's original plan
for sexuality – is desperately needed today, because our culture's native
"beat" has made us deaf to it. And no one is better suited to deliver the
invitation than Christopher West. For more than a decade he has been
"translating" the Theology of the Body for popular audiences – from
the dense and lofty language of philosophical discourse into language
and experiences we can all understand.

Because a substantial part of the book is taken up with John
Paul's reflections on the Song of Songs, anyone who reads it will
find themselves at the intersection of the sacred and the sexual. This
is especially true of the book's second half, which shows how the
conjugal union of spouses can both illuminate and be purified by the
celebration of the liturgy. The combination may seem odd, perhaps
even offensive, to some sensibilities. But the point of this book is
to teach us to see the body as the revelation of a "great mystery," to
experience the desire for intimate union as an echo of God's desire to
unite himself with us forever, and to let the one flesh union of man
and woman point us toward the mystery of Christ and the Church.

If that seems strange, I would suggest that the strangeness is not so much with the book as it is with our sensibilities. It is diagnostic. It shows how far we have drifted from the biblical worldview that includes the Song of Songs.

Anyone who has longed to break free from the culture of death, especially its twisted understanding of sexuality, will find a veritable "Declaration of Independence" in this book. Anyone who has waited for the healing that a culture of life can bring to our experience of the body and sexual desire will find the principles of a new cultural "Constitution" written in these pages.

Jesus Christ is the great healer — the divine physician — of body and soul. These reflections on the Theology of the Body and the Song of Songs contain a prescription for treating many of the wounds that sin has inflicted on our sexuality. Let the healing begin!

+ *Robert J. Carlson*

Most Reverend Robert J. Carlson,
Bishop of Saginaw

Introduction

What is it about music and song? Consider what happens when you chance upon one of your favorite songs on the radio. What emotions does it stir? What season of your life does it immediately zoom you back to? What longings does it awaken?

And all this happens because certain sound waves vibrating at a given combination of frequencies reach your ear and rattle some small pieces of bone and membrane inside your skull. *What?* Amazing!

If we ponder this phenomenon we will see how the very reality of music speaks of the profound unity of the physical and the spiritual within us as human beings. How is it that music – a resolutely physical reality – can give voice to the loftiest expressions of the human spirit, lifting our souls towards the heavens? Our ability both to compose and to appreciate music and song, in fact, is one of the clearest indications that human beings have the capacity for God. Indeed, we are made in his own image. We reflect his own glory.

Heaven's Song

Now imagine, if you can, the greatest of all songs, the pinnacle of all musical achievements. What would it do to the soul? How powerfully would it stir you? How powerfully *could* it stir you? Yet it would remain as nothing, a trifling noise compared to heaven's song.

It is reported that St. Francis of Assisi once asked God to allow him to hear the music of heaven. The Lord told Francis he knew not what he asked, for the sheer glory of heaven's song would spell certain death. The persistent saint pleaded eagerly, "Can't I hear just one note?" God conceded. As the story goes, Francis awoke from his coma a few days later.

Heaven's music is simply too much for mortals. Like the pitch that shatters glass, human beings simply cannot handle the infinitely transcendent melody of the Song that has been sung throughout eternity among the Father, the Son, and the Holy Spirit. Heaven's song needs to be transposed into a key that we mortals can actually hear and respond to. The divine Song needs to be translated into a poetic language that human beings can understand and embrace. Thanks be to God, it *has* been, and in a "way worthy of the greatest works of human genius," as Pope John Paul II has put it (TOB 111:6). In fact, the Bible claims it as *the* greatest song ever written, the song of all songs – the boldly erotic *Song of Songs*.

As we will learn throughout this book, sexual love is the earthly key that enables us to enter into heaven's song. How often does Scripture invite us to "break into song" or to "sing a new song"? What song do you think Scripture is inviting us to sing if not the greatest of all songs, the Song of Songs? As saints throughout history attest, this erotic song provides the "mystical key" that opens the "holy door" to deep union and intimacy with God. For, as Scripture teaches, the one-flesh union is a "great mystery" that refers to Christ and his union with the Church (see Eph 5:31-32). This *doesn't* mean we all need an earthly spouse in order to enter into mystical union with God. But it *does* mean that, for all of us, a pathway to a deep intimacy with God opens up as we come to understand "sexual love as it was meant to be." And *that's* the goal of this book: to use that "mystical key" of sexual love to open the holy door to union with God. Hence, this book, while focusing on themes of erotic love, is not only for married people. It is for anyone and everyone – single people, married people, and consecrated celibates – who long to sing heaven's song and thus enter more deeply into the "great mystery" of Christ's love for the Church.

Sexual Love as it Was Meant to Be

While *sexual activity* is properly the domain of spouses, *sexuality* is the domain of every human being. Jesus asks, "Have you not read that he who made them from the beginning made them male and female?" (Mt 19:4). Our maleness and femaleness – our "sexuality" – is the "fundamental fact" of human existence, according to John Paul II (see TOB 18:4). As such, our sexuality is "by no means something purely biological, but concerns the innermost being of the human person" (FC 11).

At this deepest level, as John Paul II helps us to see, God inscribed in our sexuality the vocation to love in his own image. This calling presents itself as an intense yearning for communion with an "other," a yearning that the Greeks called *eros*. Eros, however, should not be equated with lust. Lust reduces eros to a base quest for pleasure at the expense of others. While our fallen humanity certainly inclines us in this direction, John Paul II insisted that *there is another way* to live and experience erotic desire. He insisted that "the redemption of our bodies" won for us by Christ (see Rom 8:23) allows us to rediscover "that fullness of 'eros,' which implies the upward impulse of the human spirit toward what is true, good, and beautiful, so that what is 'erotic' also becomes true, good, and beautiful" (TOB 48:1).

And *that*, again, is the goal of this book – to help us experience the "fullness of eros" and, through that, to be enraptured by the mystery to which erotic love and union points: union with God himself. As Pope Benedict XVI observed, "*eros* tends to rise 'in ecstasy' toward the Divine, to lead us beyond ourselves; yet for this very reason," he added, "it calls for a path of ... purification and healing" (DC 5). This book will help you journey on this path and, I hope, help you to heal from the wounds we have all suffered living in this broken world. As human experience readily confirms, when sexual desire is misdirected, it can lead to deep pain, even despair. On the other hand, when it is properly integrated within the mystery of the person, sexual desire, as John Paul II affirmed, becomes "a vector of aspiration along which [our] whole existence develops and perfects itself from within" (LR, p. 46). *That's* what we are after in this book: discovering and living erotic desire as a channel through which we become the men and women we are created to be.

Be Not Afraid!

What is the biggest obstacle to living our sexuality as it was meant to be? Fear. We see it right in Genesis: "I was afraid, because I was naked, so I hid myself" (Gen 3:10). We long for intimacy with God and with one another, but we are often afraid of it. Like Adam, we are often afraid to reveal our true selves. Before sin, the first man and woman stood naked before God and one another without fear, without shame (see Gen 2:25). That is to say, they lived in profound *intimacy* with God and with one another.

To begin reclaiming true intimacy in our lives, we must, of course, have the courage to face our fears. Adam was afraid *because he was naked.* Here is where we must press in. The naked human body, with all the fear and intrigue surrounding it, provides precisely the clue that, if we are able to decipher it, will teach us how to sing heaven's song. It is actually at the deepest spiritual level of our sexuality – not merely the physical level – that we are "afraid" and find ourselves "hiding" from God and one another. We must allow God's perfect love to cast out that fear (see I Jn 4:18). John Paul II's Theology of the Body helps us to do just that.

John Paul II's Theology of the Body

Contrary to what many might think, John Paul II's priestly celibacy was no obstacle to his coming to understand the divine plan for sexual love. In fact, it was his priesthood that compelled him to dive ever more deeply into God's plan for the love of man and woman and to share it with others. As he himself wrote:

> I felt almost an inner call in this direction. ... *As a young priest I learned to love human love.* This has been one of the fundamental themes of my priesthood – my ministry in the pulpit, in the confessional, and also in my writing. If one loves human love, there naturally arises the need to commit oneself completely to the service of "fair love," because love is fair, it is beautiful. After all ... people are always searching for the beauty in love. They want their love to be beautiful. If they give into weakness, following [worldly] models of behavior ... in the depths of their hearts they still desire a beautiful and pure love. (CTH, pp. 122-123)

Ain't it the truth? In my high school and college years, I had given in to much weakness in this regard. Having been "evangelized" by the likes of Hugh Hefner, I followed what the world told me would satisfy the hunger within me. And I came to learn first hand that you can eat out of the dumpster only for so long before you start feeling nauseous, before you start thinking *there has got to be better food out there than this*. In the depths of my heart, just as John Paul said above, I desired a beautiful and pure love; I desired sexual love *as it was meant to be*. But I had no idea what that was, what it looked like. So I went searching.

Jesus said, "Seek, and you will find" (Lk 11:9). Making a long story short, what I eventually found was Pope John Paul II's Theology of the Body (TOB), a collection of 129 papal addresses on the meaning of our creation as male and female. I remember thinking, as I read it for the first time, that somehow I had chanced upon the long-lost treasure that every person longed for, the path to the banquet of love that truly satisfies the hungers of the human heart. Perhaps it was youthful idealism (I was just under twenty-four at the time) or delusions of grandeur, but I truly believed that somehow, for some reason, I was privy to "divine secrets" that had the potential to transform the world. I sensed then that I would spend the rest of my life studying John Paul II's mystical vision, immersing myself more deeply into it, and sharing its riches with others. Thus began my mission and career as a "theologian of the body."

The "Hidden" Talks of John Paul II

In the summer of 2005, Dr. Michael Waldstein of the International Theological Institute in Austria contacted me to ask for my assistance with a very exciting project he was working on — a fresh English translation of John Paul II's TOB. Having worked with the existing

English editions for nearly a dozen years at that point, I was well aware of their shortcomings.[1] News of Waldstein's project was music to my ears. But, as a TOB devotee, what I was about to learn knocked me off my chair.

During his research for the project, Waldstein discovered John Paul II's original manuscript in the archives in Rome. The text, Waldstein told me, was written as a lengthy book and had been divided by John Paul II into 135 talks. But, as I knew well, he had only delivered 129. *Are you kidding me?! New, undelivered material from John Paul II's Theology of the Body!?* To what shall I compare my astonishment and delight? It is like a die-hard Beatles fan finding out that some unknown tracks from the Fab Four had just been discovered in an obscure closet at Abbey Road studios. And not only that – when I finally got my hands on this new material, I realized that these lost "songs" were not "b-sides." This material had not fallen by the wayside because it wasn't up to par. This material contained some of the most beautiful tracks that John Paul (the pope, not Lennon and McCartney) had ever laid down: deeply moving reflections on the intimacy of the lovers in the Song of Songs; penetrating insights into the spiritual battle that accompanied the marriage of Tobias and Sarah in the book of Tobit; and new illuminations on the "spousal" nature of the Church's liturgy gleaned from St. Paul's teaching on the "great mystery" of marital union in Ephesians 5.

John Paul *had* delivered four addresses on these themes as part of his 129 talks. I was quite familiar with those. But Waldstein discovered that there were actually *ten* prepared talks in this section

---

[1] See Waldstein's Introduction to the TOB (pp. 11 ff.) for a discussion of these shortcomings and the need for a new translation.

of the catechesis, which the Pope had condensed into four.[2] The ten unabridged talks unearthed for the English-speaking world for the first time by Waldstein[3] offer a much fuller vision.

Heaven's Song zooms in on this section of John Paul II's catechesis – talks 108 to 117[4] – unfolding the hidden treasures of these unabridged addresses in an extended form for the first time. Although I have touched on these themes elsewhere,[5] it seemed not only appropriate but necessary to give this new content – tucked away all these years in the John Paul II archives – a fuller exposition. This is what you now hold in your hands. It is not an academic treatment of the late Pope's teaching. Rather, it is an attempt to make his wisdom accessible to a wider audience, to bring the divine secrets of John Paul's "spousal mysticism" to all those "with ears to hear."

If you are already familiar with John Paul's TOB, you will delight in this new material. If you have not been exposed to the genius of John

---

[2]   These four significantly abridged talks were delivered at the Wednesday general audiences of May 23, May 30, June 6, and June 27, 1984. See TOB pp. 548-609 for a line-by-line comparison of what was and was not delivered.

[3]   Of the many translations of the TOB, only the Polish edition, a publication overseen by Stanislaw Dziwisz (John Paul II's personal secretary) and released in 1986, contained the unabridged versions of these talks.

[4]   In this work, I draw from various other addresses in the TOB to provide context. However, it is easy to recognize the "new" material by looking for references to the numbered addresses between 108-117. Of course, if you are already familiar with the four abridged talks that John Paul did deliver, you will recognize some of the themes.

[5]   I unfolded the contents of these addresses in a more limited and more academic way in the revised edition of my commentary *Theology of the Body Explained* (Pauline, 2007). *Heaven's Song*, in fact, is a greatly expanded and more popularized version of that section of my commentary. I also touched on some of the new material in an even more limited way in the revised edition of *Theology of the Body for Beginners* (Ascension, 2008).

Paul's catechesis, this book will serve as a good introduction and will whet your appetite for more. As Waldstein wrote, and I wholeheartedly agree, the section of the TOB we will examine is "clearly one of the most important" in the whole of the Pope's catechesis (see TOB, Introduction, p. 119). It gives us an important window into what the Theology of the Body as a whole has to offer the Church and the world.

Song of Songs: The "Ecstasy" of Erotic Love

John Paul's reflections on the Song of Songs give us a concrete biblical example of the passionate joy that God desires for man and woman in their union. How quick we are in our pornographic culture to settle for the cheap bottle of wine offered at any and every corner liquor store, when in fact, as we learn in the Song of Songs, God wants to "intoxicate" us with the finest wine imaginable. For all those who would like to understand and enter into the biblical ideal of sexual love, this section of the book will provide much food for thought. It is certain to combat the widespread and erroneous notion that God and his Church are "down on sex" or that doing things the "holy" way stifles passion.

This section of the book will also shine a light on what the Church's mystical tradition provocatively describes as our call to "nuptial union" with God. Ultimately, only union with God can satisfy the deep "ache" within us for love. The intimate love of spouses is actually a sign, a *sacrament* of something infinitely greater. Those who consecrate themselves entirely to God as celibates witness to this greater union with their very lives. By doing so, they do not reject their sexuality. Rather, they show us the ultimate purpose and meaning of human sexuality: to point us to union with God.

This is why throughout history great celibate mystics have found themselves entirely at home in the erotic poetry of the Song of Songs. They see the bigger picture and, by God's grace, have entered the inner logic of the Song. Hence, we will be turning to great mystic-saints like John of the Cross, Teresa of Avila, and especially Louis de Montfort to help us unpack John Paul II's reflections on this biblical ode to erotic love.

Tobias and Sarah: The "Agony" of Erotic Love

Of course, experiencing the deep joy of marital love and union as spoken of in the Song of Songs does not come automatically. The dramatic trials that Tobias and Sarah face right from the start of their relationship demonstrate the intensity of the battle we must fight as men and women if we are to love each other as God intended "in the beginning." From the first pages of Genesis, we see that a meddling force is literally hell-bent on driving a thorny wedge between the sexes. Knowingly or unknowingly, every couple in history has felt the impact of the deceiver's schemes. John Paul II's reflections on Tobias and Sarah show us the certain path to victory in the spiritual battle that assails unsuspecting married couples everywhere. That path is to enter wholeheartedly into the "great mystery" of Christ's spousal union with the Church (see Eph 5:31-32). We do this, as we shall see, by allowing marital love and union to become a participation in the Church's liturgy.

Yes, according to John Paul II, when we experience marital union as it was meant to be experienced, it is something "liturgical" – that is, it is caught up *into the very heart* of the Church's life of prayer and worship. The Pope had already said as much in the abridged version of his reflections. The unabridged version, though, brings this idea full circle. If spousal union is "liturgical," then the Church's liturgy, John Paul shows us, is also "spousal." In other words, when we experience the Church's liturgical life as it was meant to be experienced, we experience it as the intimate union of spouses, Christ and his Church. Indeed, as we shall discover, the whole reality of the Church's prayer and sacramental-liturgical life is modeled after the loving union of spouses. It is no mere coincidence, then, that the liturgical chaos of the last several decades has coincided with a sexual chaos. The two, as we shall see more clearly, are profoundly linked.

Real-Life Stories: From Theory to Practice

These are "mystical" ideas – that is, ideas that bring us face-to-face with *great mysteries*. That's what theology is meant to do. But theological ideas, if they are to do more than tickle our intellects, must be applied in our everyday lives. In order to help pave the way from theory to practice, I set the stage for each chapter with a story. At the end of each chapter, I conclude the story, demonstrating how various themes of that chapter apply in this real-life situation. While I have fictionalized all of the names and many of the details, these stories are all based on real events and exchanges I have had with individuals and couples over the years. These stories expose gritty, painful issues in a way that readers of "pious" books might not expect. True to life, they are not all "victory stories." Not all end happily. But each shows how John Paul II's teaching is of critical importance where it matters most – in those dark, broken places of our lives that desperately need God's healing light. My hope is that each of these stories will inspire you to persevere through whatever trials you may be facing on the road to holiness.

As we will see, the road to holiness passes by way of sexual
healing and integration. The way we understand our bodies and
the union of man and woman has a direct bearing on the way we
understand Christ's body and his union with the Church (see Eph
5:31-32). Hence, if we are to *enter in* to proper union with Christ and
his Church, the diseased images and ideas we have about our own
bodies and sexual union *must* be healed. It can be a long and painful
journey – and there is no detour. Reflection questions at the end of
each chapter are intended to aid the reader in a prayerful examination
of ideas and attitudes that may keep us from a proper vision of our
bodies and sexuality.

Odd as it may seem to some, a proper vision of our sexuality
(the fruit of integration) provides the clearest window for catching a
glimpse of the "great mystery" of God's ultimate plan for our lives and
the universe. Conversely, a distorted vision of our sexuality serves as
one of the most effective *blocks* to understanding who God really is, who
we really are, and what the "great mystery" of Christianity is really all
about. No wonder the enemy so viciously attacks our sexuality!

A Delicate Task

Lucifer is the great plagiarizer. He takes what belongs to Christ
and puts his own name on it, claiming the erotic realm for himself.
Tragically, it seems many Christians are content to let him have it.
It is not uncommon to encounter people who – in the name of a
supposed "piety" – find the very idea of linking erotic love and Christ's
love unconscionable. In adopting this attitude, however, we do not
overcome the deceiver's lies; we unwittingly buy into them. *We must not
surrender the erotic realm to the enemy!* We *must not* let his distortions bind us

to our own lusts and blind us to the "great mystery" revealed through our bodies! Precarious as it is, we *must* be courageous in reclaiming the erotic sphere for Christ and his Church. For, as both Old and New Testaments teach us – and as we see especially in the Song of Songs – the erotic sphere is the privileged realm of a divine revelation.

Reclaiming the erotic sphere for Christ does not mean, of course, that we bring eros back "as is" from the enemy's turf. Rightly do the pious recoil at this idea. For appealing to the lustful distortions of our sexuality as images of the divine would be blasphemy. Rather, in the process of reclaiming the erotic realm for Christ, we must submit all that is "erotic" to a radical transformation. This process of transformation is an uncertain and fragile journey, but it is one made possible by grace (see VS 18). I encourage you to embark on this journey with bold confidence in God's healing power, but also with a realistic appraisal of the hazards involved. In Dante's *Divine Comedy*, along the narrow terrace of purgation from lust, we hear this just warning: "Be sure to keep your eyes straight on course, for one could slip here easily and fall'" (Purgatorial Canto 25).

Describing divine mysteries with sexual imagery is tricky business – especially in our culture, immersed as it is in a terribly distorted vision of the body and sex. When treated without care and attention – or, when put into the wrong hands – the supremely holy and sacred can quickly degenerate into the crude and profane. There is wisdom in the ancient Jewish tradition that forbade reading of the Song of Songs before a demonstrated level of maturity. John Paul himself, according to his long-time secretary Stanislaw Cardinal Dziwisz, did not deliver the full text of his teaching on the Song of Songs precisely because its content was "too delicate" for a general audience in which young ears would be present.[6] Suffice it to say, I am writing this book for a mature readership and presupposing a high level of purity in the reader. For one man's mystical treasure can be another man's occasion of sin, and I certainly do not want to lead anyone into the latter.

Test Everything

Of course, we carry these treasures in earthen vessels. As an author, I do not suppose that in discussing these mysteries I have hit the nail on the head with precisely the right tone, qualification, and nuance. That is an art I have yet to perfect. Inevitably, though, this book will wind up in the hands of some who will object, not just to imperfections, but to the very idea of applying intimate, erotic imagery to the things of God. On the one hand, acknowledging my own fallibility, I would say to such readers (as to all readers): "Test everything; hold fast [only to] what is good" (1 Thess 5:21). On the other hand, I would humbly ask those who may find themselves uncomfortable with the imagery in this book to examine the possibility that their own heart might be in need of healing and integration.

We are often prone to what John Paul II called "the interpretation of suspicion" (see TOB 46), an attitude that cannot imagine any prism other than lust through which to see or discuss erotic matters. Lust is certainly a powerful force that can cloud and even dominate our thinking. However, as John Paul II insisted, we *"cannot stop at casting the heart into a state of* continual and irreversible *suspicion* due to

---

6   Michael Waldstein and I met with Cardinal Dziwisz in Krakow on March 12, 2008 to pose various questions to him about John Paul II's TOB, including why John Paul II did not deliver his full text on the Song of Songs.

the manifestations of [lust] ... Redemption is a truth, a reality, in the name of which man must feel himself called, and 'called with effectiveness'" (TOB 46:4). This means that God's grace, through its power to heal and transform us inwardly, can lead us to a *pure* way of seeing and thinking about our bodies and the gift of our sexuality. As the *Catechism* teaches, "Even now [purity of heart] enables us to see *according to* God ... it lets us perceive the human body – ours and our neighbor's – as a temple of the Holy Spirit, a manifestation of divine beauty" (CCC 2519).

That is what we are after in this book. To get there, we must be willing to persevere in following Christ through each of the different stages of the interior life. In the Prologue, I present a marvelous excerpt from John Paul II's last published work in which he outlines this journey and what we can expect in its different stages. I strongly encourage you to spend some time with it. It is only by persevering beyond the initial and essentially purgative stage of this journey that we come to experience God's light illuminating "the gratuitous beauty of the human body" as a sign of his own Mystery and of our call to "nuptial union" with him.

My simple hope and prayer is that the Lord will use the words and images of this book, despite their many inadequacies, to open hidden doorways for you into these heavenly places. If those doorways open – *be not afraid to enter!* Beauty beyond imagining lies within.

– Christopher West

The Journey of the Interior Life

J ohn Paul II's book *Memory and Identity*, his final published work
before his death, provides a concise and beautifully expressed
picture of the three stages of the interior life. Perseverance on the
journey that John Paul II outlines below is critical if we are to enter
beyond the "scandal" of the Song of Songs and into the depth of
mystical meaning found in its erotic imagery.

> In the mystery of Redemption, Christ's victory over
> evil is given to us ... as a task. We accept that task as
> we set out upon the way of the interior life, working
> consciously on ourselves – with Christ as our Teacher.
> The Gospel calls us to follow this very path ...
>
> The call "Follow me!" is an invitation to set out
> along the path to which the inner dynamic of the
> mystery of Redemption leads us. This is the path
> indicated by the teaching, so often found in the writings
> on the interior life and on mystical experience, about
> the three stages involved in "following Christ" ... We
> speak of the purgative way, the illuminative way, and the
> unitive way. In reality, these are not three distinct ways,
> but three aspects of the same way, along which Christ

calls everyone, as he once called the young man in the Gospel.

... Observance of the commandments, properly understood, is synonymous with the purgative way: it means conquering sin, moral evil in its various guises. And this leads to gradual inner purification.

It also enables us to discover values. And hence we conclude that the purgative way leads organically into the illuminative way. Values are lights which illuminate existence and, as we work on our lives, they shine ever more brightly on the horizon. So side by side with observance of the commandments – which has an essentially purgative meaning – we develop virtues. For example, in observing the commandment: "You shall not kill!" we discover the value of life under various aspects and we learn an ever deeper respect for it. In observing the commandment: "You shall not commit adultery!" we acquire the virtue of purity, and this means that we come to an ever greater awareness of the gratuitous beauty of the human body, of masculinity and femininity. This gratuitous beauty becomes a light for our actions ...

So the illuminative stage in the interior life emerges gradually from the purgative stage. With the passage of time, if we persevere in following Christ our Teacher, we feel less and less burdened by the struggle against sin, and we enjoy more and more the divine light which pervades all creation. This is most important, because it allows us to escape from a situation of constant inner exposure to the risk of sin — even though, on this earth, the risk always remains present to some degree — so as to move with ever greater freedom within the whole created world. This same freedom and simplicity characterizes our relations with other human beings, including those of the opposite sex. Interior light illumines our actions and shows us all the good in the created world as coming from the hand of God.

Thus the purgative way and then the illuminative way form the organic introduction to what is known as the unitive way. This is the final stage of the interior journey, when the soul experiences a special union with God. This union is realized in contemplation of the divine Being and in the experience of love which flows from it with growing intensity. In this way we somehow anticipate what is destined to be ours in eternity, beyond death and the grave. Christ, supreme Teacher of the spiritual life, together with all those who have been formed in his school, teaches that even in this life we can enter onto the path of union with God.

[To the degree that we enter this unitive way we] can find God in everything, we can commune with him in and through all things. Created things cease to be a danger for us as once they were, particularly while we were still at the purgative stage of our journey. Creation, and other people in particular, not only regain their true light, given to them by God the Creator, but, so to speak, they lead us to God himself, in the way that he willed to

reveal himself to us: as Father, Redeemer, and Spouse.
(MI, pp. 27-39)

It seems that many teachers of the faith imply that the purgative stage of the journey is all we can realistically expect in this life, as if a life of "virtue" meant no more than learning how to restrain ourselves from sin by force of will. Here, John Paul II shows us that, if we persevere in following Christ, we can and should expect more, much more! In fact, settling for less can be a form of sinfulness. The Spirit desires – longs! – for us to grow to full maturity in Christ.

In the language of St. Thomas Aquinas, a person who can successfully restrain himself from sin is "continent," but not yet *virtuous*. Continence falls short of virtue since virtue presupposes a right desire, and this is lacking in the continent person (see *Summa, Prima Secundae*, q. 58, a. 3, ad 2). As the *Catechism* keenly observes, "The perfection of the moral good consists in man's being moved to the good not only by his will but also by his 'heart'" and even "by his sensitive appetite" (CCC 1770, 1775). Human virtues do not suppress or tyrannize our passions. They "order our passions ... They make possible ease, self-mastery, and joy in leading a morally good life" (CCC 1804).

Continual growth in virtue is a task of the Christian life. Let us, at John Paul II's invitation, "accept that task." Whatever our particular difficulties and trials might be, let us persevere in following Christ our Teacher "so as to move with ever greater freedom within the whole created world." This book aims to assist you in that task.

Part I

The Song of Songs

Chapter 1

The Biblical Ode to Erotic Love

Ellen, now in her early thirties, recalls with tears the day of her first menses. She had just turned thirteen. Her parents, "good Catholics" from all external appearances, had told her next to nothing about her developing body or what to expect, so she had no idea what was happening to her. She was terrified and thought she needed to go to the hospital, but she was too afraid to say anything to her parents. Everything that had to do with *those* parts of the body was clouded in shame in the Dawson family. Nobody talked about it – ever. Except to scold. She remembers having her hand slapped in the bathtub when she was five, with her mother shouting, "Don't *ever* touch yourself there!"

Now she was bleeding from "there." What was she supposed to do? A day later, she called her best friend in a panic. Her friend's mother got on the phone and tried to calm her down. She began to explain to Ellen what was happening – that it was perfectly natural, and that she was developing into the woman God created her to be.

God ...? What does God have to do with this? she remembers thinking. The only thing she could imagine, based on her "religious" upbringing, was that God was very displeased with her. What *does* God have to do with this? Only now, twenty years later, after much pain and suffering, is Ellen beginning to understand the answer to that question.

W hy is the Song of Songs the favorite biblical book of the mystics? Why have the saints written more commentaries on this seemingly obscure and wildly erotic love poetry than on any other book in the Bible? Hmmm ... What do they know that most Christians seem not to? If this is "heaven's song" transposed into a human key, then, as the saints and mystics know, the Song of Songs is the authentic soundtrack of Christianity.

The Church has an incredibly joyful song to sing. It is the song of the Bride rejoicing in total surrender to the love of her Bridegroom. "It is the utter depth of love that produces [her] singing," Pope Benedict tells us. Then he quotes St. Augustine: "'*Cantare amantis est*'... singing is a lover's thing." The Church's love song, in fact, is "the new tongue that comes from the Holy Spirit." In this heavenly song, says Benedict, the Church experiences "an inebriation surpassing all the possibilities of mere rationality" (SL, pp. 140, 142). In other words, we cannot enter the joy – the "inebriation" – of the Church's love song merely with our minds, merely with an intellectual, rational grasp of theological ideas, however "correct" those ideas might be. Singing comes from a different "place" within the human being: from the depths of the heart.

The Bride's True Song

Our Bridegroom's "steadfast love and faithfulness" should cause us to "break forth into joyous song" (Ps 98:3-4). Yet, how many of us are embarrassed to sing, let alone "sing joyfully," especially in front of others? Singing exposes our hearts, makes us vulnerable. So we tend to lock up our hearts and cling to "mere rationality" out of fear of the Bride's true song — out of fear, that is, of *the Song of Songs*. As a result, the Christian message is often set to the wrong music, or it is not set to music at all. When this happens, Christianity becomes dry, cold, and seemingly irrelevant to the real desires of our hearts. In fact, when Christian teaching is set to the wrong music, it can even come across as an affront to our hearts.

I remember one Sunday morning praying in church after Mass. It was a particularly graced time and, in my own limited way, I was hearing "the Song of Songs" deep in my heart. My delight was rudely interrupted, however, by the scolding tones of a religion teacher instructing some children about the real presence of Christ in the tabernacle. What she was saying about Christ was technically correct, but her harsh, condescending approach set the whole message to the wrong music. It was like somebody took the needle on the record of the Song of Songs and abruptly scratched it across the surface. *Mercy, God!* I thought. *There goes another generation of disaffected Catholics* ...

I am convinced that much of today's rebellion against Christianity — especially Christian teaching on sexuality — stems from the fact that the Gospel message, in most of our upbringings, has been set to the wrong music. For example, people today often confuse Christian purity with puritanism — which, as we shall see, plays a *very different* tune, one that is tragically *out of tune* with the Song of Songs.

Purity vs. Puritanism

John Paul II observes that in the whole history of literature and art, in the history of human culture, the subject of erotic love *seems to be particularly frequent* and is *particularly important* (see TOB 63:3). Human existence is simply incomprehensible without the passion that draws man and woman towards each other and ultimately toward their climactic union in "one flesh." This dramatic union of the two – both earthy and otherwordly – is the foundation stone of human life itself.

This is why the whole sphere of erotic love, as John Paul says, "has been, is, and will be the subject of literary narrative." Thus, it should not surprise us that such a narrative "found its place also in the Bible ... in the text of the Song of Songs" (TOB 63:3). Those who *are* surprised to find an unabashed celebration of erotic love in the Bible have most likely confused Christian purity with puritanism. Christian purity sees "the glory of God in the human body" (TOB 57:3). Puritanism, on the other hand, sees only the foul stain of sin. Puritanism considers the soul as the "good" part of us and the body as the "bad" part. *Such thinking couldn't be further from an authentic Christian perspective!*

The idea that the human body is "bad" is actually a *heresy* (a blatant error explicitly condemned by the Church) known as Manichaeism. Mani (or Manichaeus), after whom this false teaching is named, condemned the body and all things sexual because he saw the material world as the source of evil. But Scripture teaches that everything God created is "very good" (see Gen 1:31) and that nothing should be rejected when received from God with thanksgiving (see 1 Tim 4:4). John Paul II summarized the essential distinction as follows: While the Manichaean mentality assigns an "anti-value" to the body and sexuality, Christianity teaches that the body and sexuality "always remain 'a value not sufficiently appreciated'" (TOB 45:3). In other words, whereas Manichaeism says "the body is bad," Christianity says "the body is so good that you can't even fathom it."

For those locked in a puritanical or Manichaean perspective, it is simply impossible to understand the Song of Songs. As John Paul observes, to many this book has seemed "profane." Its reading has often been discouraged and even forbidden (see TOB 108:2). "Merciful God, how great is our stupidity!" laments Saint Teresa of Avila, in response to those who disparage the Song of Songs (cited in CL, p. 42). Let us recall St. Paul's words, "To the pure, all things are pure" (Titus 1:15). With just such purity, the greatest saints and mystics have drawn lasting inspiration from this sacred, erotic poetry and the Magisterium of the Church has inserted its verses into the liturgy (see TOB 108:2). One must understand that this mystical and liturgical tradition – rather than the parallel history of fear and suspicion – reflects *the authentic mind of the Church* regarding the Song of Songs. For as the Church prays, so does she believe.

God Wants to "Marry" Us

The burning verses of this erotic Song speak to the jubilation that authentic Christian purity affords. "Blessed are the pure in heart, for they shall see God" (Mt 5:8). How can we, mere mortals, "see God"? Impossible! But purity, as a gift from God, makes it possible to catch a glimpse. Purity enables us to see something of the mystery of God and live! What joy, what rapture, what blessed, bounteous bliss! And if we understand what John Paul II has given us in his TOB, we can add this: Purity enables us to see a sign of God's mystery *through the human body and the mystery of sexual difference.* For the "body, in fact, and only the body, is capable of making visible ... the mystery hidden from eternity in God." And it does so precisely through our "'visible' masculinity and femininity" (TOB 19:4).

If we allow the Song of Songs to resonate in us, we will realize that the body and sexuality are not only biological realities. They are also, and even more so, *theological* realities. They reveal the "great mystery" of God and his plan to unite himself with us forever. "'For this reason a man shall leave his father and mother and be joined to his wife, and the two shall become one flesh.' This is a great mystery, and I mean in reference to Christ and the church" (Eph 5:31–32).

John Paul describes this passage from Ephesians as "the compendium or *summa*, in some sense, *of the teaching about God and man* which was brought to fulfillment by Christ" (LF 19). In other words, if you are looking for a passage that summarizes the entire message of the Bible, the whole teaching about who God is and who we are — this one fits the bill quite nicely. And it is all about how sexual union points us (or, at least, is meant to point us) to union with God. Of all the images and analogies used by Scripture to help us understand the mystery of God's love, this is the primary one. In Sacred Scripture, *eros* (human, erotic love) is meant to reveal and express *agape* (divine, sacrificial love).

Of course, like all analogies, the biblical analogy of erotic love and spousal union cannot possibly explain the divine mystery fully. God's mystery remains infinitely transcendent (see TOB 95b:1). And yet, as John Paul stated, "There is no other human reality which corresponds more, humanly speaking, to that divine mystery" (Homily, Dec 30, 1988).

Think about it: from beginning to end the Bible tells the story of marriage. It begins with the marriage of *the first* Adam and Eve in Genesis and ends with the marriage of *the final* Adam and Eve, Christ and the Church, in the book of Revelation. And if you bring those two marriages together to meet in the middle of the story, guess where you will land? If your Bible is, say, 1200 pages, you will find the Song of Songs right about page 600. The fact that the Song of Songs is in the *center* of the Bible seems much more than a coincidence. It speaks – or, rather, it *sings* – quite loudly of the Bible's central message: God loves us passionately, intimately, like a bridegroom loves his bride. God rejoices in us! He exults over his people "with loud singing" (Zeph 3:17).

What kind of singing? If it is "heaven's song," it must be the greatest of all songs. In other words, it must be ... the *Song of Songs*. Since the dawn of creation, God has been singing to us, wooing us, enticing us, calling us, inviting us. And if we listen to the enchanting melody and unabashedly erotic lyrics of his Song, we will understand that God *longs* to "marry" us. We will understand that God's eternal plan is to espouse us to himself forever (see Hos 2:19) so that we might share in the bliss of his own eternal Communion of love.

As the *Catechism of the Catholic Church* proclaims: "God himself is an eternal exchange of love ... and he has destined us to share in that exchange" (CCC 221). One of the critical illuminations of John Paul II's TOB – in keeping, of course, with the great mystical tradition of the Church – is that this divine secret is whispered in and through the true language of erotic love. God's mysterious plan is not "out there" somewhere. It could not be any closer to us. It is *right here*, mysteriously re-presented in our very being as male and female. Right from the beginning, the marriage of man and woman was meant to be a "sign," a "sacrament" of the marriage to be consummated in heaven, the marriage of Christ and the Church. As St. John of the Cross put it – every human being is invited to "mystical marriage" with God. God sets forth his marriage proposal and patiently awaits the response of the bride. With her freely given "yes" – and only with her freely given "yes" – the heavenly Bridegroom rejoices to pour his eternal, immortal, invisible seed (his Word) within her, filling her, "impregnating" her with divine life.

Christians realize that this is not mere poetry. A young Jewish woman heard this divine song, this wedding proposal, and *sang back* with such openness to God's gift that she literally conceived divine life in her womb. "And the Word was made flesh" (Jn 1:14). As St. Louis de Montfort put it, God sent his angel to Mary "in order to win her heart." And on account of the "hidden delights" of his divine proposal, "she gave her consent." At that moment, God poured a "chalice of ambrosia" into the womb of his virgin bride and, opening to this "divine nectar," she conceived God's own Son. Such imagery would have been enough to give my wonderful but rather prudish grandmother cardiac arrest. For anyone experiencing palpitations, de Montfort reminds us plainly: "These are comparisons made by the saints" (TD, nn. 252-253) – saints who, undoubtedly, were immersed in the holy imagery of the Song of Songs.

It is with good reason that the Song of Songs is the favorite biblical book of so many of the mystics. Mystics are not dreamy believers out of touch with reality; they, in fact, are the ones potently *in touch* with Reality. They are men and women *madly* in love with God and burning to know him ever more deeply. They are men and women who have heard the divine love song and learned, through many purifying trials and tribulations, to sing back and harmonize with the Trinity. For such men and women, the erotic love poetry of the Song provides a language – certainly inadequate but, as many saints have discovered, the *least* inadequate – for expressing their own experience of God's passionate love and their panting for more of it. St. Augustine describes this yearning in his *Confessions*: "You breathed your fragrance on me; I drew in breath and now I pant for you. I have tasted you, now I hunger and thirst for more. You touched me, and I burned for your peace."

Interpreting the Song of Songs

It is obvious to any student of Scripture that the poetry of the Song is connected in some way with the whole biblical tradition of the spousal analogy. It certainly serves to illuminate the prophets' description of God's spousal love for Israel. In turn, as so many saints and mystics attest, the Song of Songs also sheds light on Christ's spousal relationship with the Church. Interestingly enough, however, John Paul concludes that the *"theme of spousal love* in this singular biblical 'poem' lies *outside that great analogy*. The love of bridegroom and bride in the Song of Songs is a theme by itself, and in this lies the singularity and originality of that book" (TOB 108:1).

John Paul expands on this idea in four extensive footnotes. Quoting from various scholars, the Holy Father is critical of those who rush to disembody the Song, seeing it only as an allegory of God's "spiritual" love. It is "the conviction of a growing number of exegetes," the Pope maintains, that the Song of Songs (quoting biblical scholar J. Winandy) is "to be taken simply as what it manifestly is: a song of human love" (TOB 108: note 95). For "human love, created and blessed by God, can be the theme of an inspired biblical book" (TOB

108: note 97). John Paul seems to agree with the view of Alonso-Schöckel that those who have "forgotten the lovers" or "petrified them into pretense" have not interpreted the Song correctly. "'He who does not believe in the human love of the spouses, he who must ask forgiveness for the body, does not have the right to rise higher....With the affirmation of human love, by contrast, it is possible to discover the revelation of God in it'" (TOB 108: note 96).

This confirms an essential element of Christian faith. Grace – the mystery of God's life and love – is communicated *through* the "stuff" of our humanity, not despite it. We need not shed our skin in order to reach the transcendent God, as some religions (and even some misguided Christians) believe. For, in an act of total self-emptying, the transcendent God came down to our level and literally took our skin upon him. This means that right "from the beginning," our bodies have had the God-given ability to reveal divine mysteries. Thus, in reading the Song of Songs, we need not jump immediately to the spiritual and divine reality. Rather, we can and should linger on the truth of the body and the love of the spouses, allowing these to "speak." For the language of the body, according to John Paul II, is "prophetic." It proclaims the very mystery of God (see TOB 104-106). Thus, as John Paul says, quoting from yet another scholar, "a faithful and happy human love reveals to human beings the attributes of divine love" (TOB 108: note 97).

As with all of Scripture, we must find the proper balance between the human and the divine elements in the Song of Songs, holding them together in a potent fruitfulness. For the content of the Song is at one and the same time sexual and sacred. When we ignore the sacred, we see the Song merely as a secular erotic poem. But when we ignore the sexual, we see the Song merely as an allegory of "spiritual" love and fall into *allegorism*. "It is only by putting these two aspects together that one can read the book in the right way" (TOB 108: note 97).

And this is precisely what we shall attempt to do as we continue exploring John Paul's teaching on the Song of Songs. The Pope's analysis, however, isn't an exhaustive commentary. He offers reflections, rather, on some key themes of the Song with the goal of demonstrating the authentic biblical meaning of marital love and sexual union. "For such reflections, the Song of Songs has an altogether singular significance" (TOB 113:6).

Ellen's upbringing – in which the body was taboo and God and sex were antithetical – set her up for a tragic fall. She got pregnant at sixteen and, fearing her parents reaction, had an abortion. The pain and isolation of that experience drove her into a string of broken relationships and one-night stands. She became pregnant again at twenty-eight and lost the baby through a miscarriage.

It was at this point that someone gave her a book on John Paul II's Theology of the Body. It sat on her shelf for several months before she mustered up the courage to read it. After all, it was a *Catholic* book. In her mind, that could only mean one thing: she would feel scolded and shamed all over again for the life she had lived. Instead, she says, "I couldn't believe it. I found hope. For the first time in my life I began to realize that it is good, *it is good* to be a woman. There's a reason for it – a beautiful reason for it. I had just never heard it. And I was raised in a Catholic home. I went to Catholic school. Why didn't anybody ever tell me this!?"

Ellen has been in spiritual direction for almost four years now. Her director, a priest well known for guiding people through healing prayer, has helped her bring Christ's light into many of her most painful memories. One very healing exercise he led her through was to reflect on the Stations of the Cross, but to put herself in the place of Jesus – for Jesus mysteriously relives his journey to Calvary in each one of us: When was she "condemned to death"? When did she "fall" for the first time? Where did she encounter Mary on her journey? Who was "Veronica" in her life? Who was "Simon" helping her to carry her cross? When was she "stripped," etc.? Realizing that all of her sufferings can be united with Christ has helped her enter into the living hope of resurrection. "Memories remain," she says. "But they don't sting as much. I'm beginning to heal."

Although Ellen is still working through layers of bitterness towards her parents, she is learning how to forgive them and release them to God's mercy. "I'm realizing that they weren't able to give me a proper understanding of my body because no one had given it to them. In their own way, they've also suffered for lack of knowledge of God's plan." She is also learning how to forgive the men who have used her and wounded her. Perhaps even more importantly, she is learning how to forgive herself for her own failings. "The whole time [in all those relationships] I was looking for Jesus, I was looking for the Bridegroom, like the woman at the well [in John's gospel]. I know that now," she says through her tears. "But it's still so painful. I want to do whatever I can to help spare other people this pain."

Reflection Questions

I. Was there open, honest, healthy conversation in your upbringing about the beauty and glory of God's plan for making us male and female? If not, where did you learn about sex and what did you learn about it? How does what you learned measure up with what you are now learning about God's plan?

2. What were some of your earliest perceptions about your own body as a boy/girl? How have those impressions shaped your perceptions of yourself now as a man/woman?

3. Where might you be in need of replacing diseased ideas about the body and sex (your own body, and that of others) with the beauty of God's plan?

Suggested Prayer

Come Holy Spirit of truth. Give me the eyes to see the mystery of God revealed through my body and the beauty of the opposite sex. Give me the grace to confront the lies I have believed, the lies that have lodged in my heart that make it difficult for me to love, accept, and understand my body as you created it to be. Dislodge these lies from my heart that I might behold the body of Christ without shame. For therein – in Christ's body exposed and given up for me – the truth is told and Satan's lies are defeated. Therein I discover the redemption of my own body. Let it be, Lord, according to your Word. Amen.

Chapter 2

Mutual Fascination with the Body

Bill was eleven years old when he first discovered a stash of *Playboy* magazines under his older brother's bed. He can still remember the incredible rush of adrenalin that gripped him when he saw for the first time what a naked woman looked like. It awakened in him desires he had no idea he had. Revisiting the "stash" became an obsession. Later in his teen years, viewing pornography became a full-fledged addiction. He convinced himself he would stop looking at porn once he got married. And he did ... for about three months.

Eighteen years later, Bill still remembers what he calls the "disappointment" of his wedding night: "Linda [my wife] was the first real woman I had ever seen naked. We even did the 'good Christian thing' and saved sex for marriage. Not that we were totally chaste, but we pretty much kept our clothes on during our engagement. I was expecting she would look like all the thousands of naked women I had seen in magazines and movies. What a letdown. So I went back to the porn. It's been a constant struggle."

John Paul observes that it is impossible to interpret the Song of Songs outside the context of the book of Genesis and of that "primordial enchantment" that the first man and woman experienced in each other's presence (see TOB 108:3). This primordial enchantment reveals a yearning and desire planted in all of us by that mysterious "breath" that God breathed into our humanity at the dawn of time (see Gen 2:7). Upon seeing the woman God created, Adam declared, "This at last is bone of my bones and flesh of my flesh'" (Gen 2:23). These words "express wonder and admiration, or even better, the sense of fascination" (TOB 108:5). Having named all the animal-bodies and not found in those bodies the revelation of a person whom he could love, Adam's declaration seems to say, "*Look, a body that expresses the 'person'!*" (TOB 14:4). "Look, the beauty that completes me by revealing to me my beauty!"

John Paul describes Adam's original fascination with woman as the biblical prototype of the Song of Songs (see TOB 9:1). What "was barely expressed in the second chapter of Genesis ... in just a few simple and essential words is developed here in a full dialogue" (TOB 108:5). In the Song, the lovers express the same sentiments of Genesis in a complementary duet in which the bridegroom's words are interwoven with the bride's. A wonder, admiration, and fascination similar to Adam's runs "in a peaceful and even wave from the beginning to the end of the poem" (TOB 108:5). And just like Genesis, their words of love are "concentrated on the 'body.'" The "point of departure as well as the point of arrival for [their] fascination – reciprocal wonder and admiration – are in fact the bride's femininity and the bridegroom's masculinity, in the direct experience of their visibility" (TOB 108:6). The body reveals the person and the body summons them to love. This is the "incarnational principle" – namely, that the divine Spirit of Love, the Spirit of holy desire, yearns to manifest itself "in the flesh." Love seeks incarnation, to become flesh. Love is revealed *through the body*.

Think about it: a man's body does not make sense by itself. Nor does a woman's. Seen in light of each other, we discover the unmistakable plan of the Creator: man is designed for woman and woman is designed for man. We go together. Our bodies literally fit together, summoning us to the ascent of love and enabling us to be a life-giving "gift" to one another. John Paul II calls this incarnate discovery of the divine plan of love the "spousal meaning of the body." Spousal love is the love of *total* self-donation. It is *"precisely that love in which the human person becomes a gift* and – through this gift – fulfills the very meaning of his being and existence" (TOB 15:1). We are all called to love as Christ loves, and Christ's love is a *spousal* kind of love – the love of total self-giving. Hence, what we learn in the Song of Songs is not only for married people. It is for anyone and everyone who wants to learn how to love as Christ loves. This is why countless celibate saints have drawn their deepest inspiration from the erotic poetry of the Song.

Looking with Lust vs. Seeing with Love

In the inspired duet of this Song, the lovers not only "look" at each other's bodies. They *see* each others' bodies as the revelation of a "great mystery" – the mystery of the human person made in the image of God and called to love as God loves. The attraction of each lover towards the other's body is an attraction toward the other person *as a person*, not as an object to be consumed or appropriated. And seeing *the other as a person*, they do not use the person as an object of selfish gratification. Rather, as John Paul says, this attraction which lingers directly and immediately on the body *generates love* in the inner impulse of their hearts (see TOB 108:6).

While attraction toward the body is *meant* to generate love in the heart, tragically, as the experience of fallen men and women attests, the human body often generates *lust*. Lust is inverted sexual desire, sexual desire turned in on itself. When lust flares up and is given sway, it overtakes the mind and the body with adamant demands for an outlet. When that "outlet" becomes another person, we are not loving that person. Rather, we are *using* that person as a means of selfish gratification. This is an experience *very different* from the one celebrated in the Song of Songs.

Throughout the TOB, the Pope vigorously upholds the *real power* of redemption to liberate the human heart from the domination of lust, calling men and women to a new "ethos." We can recognize that the word *ethos* is related to the word *ethic*, but there is an important difference. An ethic is an external norm – "do this, don't do that." Ethos refers to a person's inner world of values. It is concerned with the desires of the human heart, with what attracts and repulses us. The Gospel calls us to a new way of seeing, thinking about, and experiencing sexual desire. Authentic Christian ethos is not marked by repression of sexual desire, but rather by its *redemption*. Redemption is related to the Latin word *redimere* which means "to ransom" or "to regain." What needs to be regained in the sexual sphere is God's original plan for sexual desire. As John Paul II wrote, "Christian ethos is characterized by *a transformation of the human person's conscience and attitudes ... such as to express and realize the value of the body and sex* according to the Creator's original plan" (TOB 45:3).

"In the beginning," God created us with a sexual desire that was the very power to love as he loves. In other words, before sin entered the world, *eros* (human, erotic love) was infused with *agape* (divine, sacrificial love). Using a biblical image, we could say that "in the beginning" the man and woman were inebriated by God's wine. Wine is a symbol of divine love poured out. What happened with the original sin? The spouses "ran out of wine." Lust is the result. Lust is eros cut off from agape. But what was Christ's first miracle? He came to the wedding feast at Cana and restored the wine in superabundance! If we drink deeply from this "new wine" we will find ourselves empowered to love as God loves, like the lovers in this great Song. But not, of course, without an ongoing and lively interior battle.

St. Paul vividly describes this interior battle in Romans 7. That which we want to do, we don't do and that which we do not want to do, we do. But Paul also cries out in thanks to Jesus Christ who saves him from this wretched situation (see Rom 7:25). Even if the battle to love rightly is fierce, there is a power at work within us that is able to do far more than we ever think or imagine (see Eph 3:20). The lovers of the Song live from "within" this power to such an extent that, as John Paul observes, it is as if they experience an ideal world in which the struggle between good and evil – love and lust – did not exist (see TOB 115:2). "The words, movements, and gestures of the spouses, their whole behavior, correspond to the inner movement of their hearts" (TOB 108:4). And the inner movement of their hearts is a pure flame of love. They are overflowing with wine, drunk with a holy inebriation. For right from the first verses of the Song, "the king" had taken his lover into his private chambers – or, better translated, into his *wine cellar* (see v. 4).

In the allegorical sense of the Song, we, of course, are the "bride" invited into God's wine cellar. What should the bride do upon entering this secret chamber? "Well, then," as Teresa of Avila says, "let her drink as much as she desires and get drunk on all these wines in the cellar of God! Let her enjoy these joys … and not fear to lose her life through drinking much more than her weak nature enables her to do. Let her die at last in this paradise of delights; blessed death that makes one live in such a way!" (cited in CL, p. 71).

In this "blessed death" of holy intoxication, sexual desire passes-over from lust to an immeasurable love. And it is precisely this drunkenness, this inner "truth and strength of love," as John Paul says, that wins the victory for man in his struggle with evil (see TOB 115:2). The more we allow God's "wine" (the Holy Spirit, see Eph 5:18) to purify our hearts through holy drunkenness, the more we experience a "real and deep victory" over the distortion of lust (see TOB 45:4). And the more we experience a "real and deep victory" over lust, the more we experience that same sense of wonder and fascination at the human sexual-body that is present in the verses of the Song of Songs — an experience *very different* from the mere arousal of lust. It is not possible to return to the state of original innocence, but it is possible for love to win in its battle with lust.

Experience of the Beautiful

Fascination with the human body in its masculinity and femininity — often considered innately prurient — is here, in the Song of Songs, a means "for training in righteousness" (2 Tim 3:16), that is, for training in *love*. Fascination with each other's bodies is, for the lovers of the Song, "a primordial and essential sign of holiness" (TOB 109:2). How often has the body been tragically cast as the enemy of holiness — as if we somehow needed to reject our bodies in the name of holiness? Nothing could be further from an authentic *Christian* understanding of holiness.

Christian holiness, by its very nature, is always *incarnational* holiness.

Biblical admonitions about the dangers of "the flesh" do not condemn the body itself. Rather, they warn us precisely about the dangers of divorcing the body from the life of holiness, of separating the body from the life of the Holy Spirit. We are not to reject our bodies, but rather to open them to the indwelling of the Holy Spirit "so that the life of Jesus may be manifested in our mortal flesh" (2 Cor 4:11). As St. Paul also says, "If the Spirit of him who raised Jesus from the dead dwells in you, he who raised Christ Jesus from the dead will give life *to your mortal bodies also* through his Spirit who dwells in you" (Rom 8:11).

By opening our bodies to the Holy Spirit, we learn how to make of our bodies "a living sacrifice" to God (see Rom 12:1). Holiness, as John Paul expressed it, is what "permits man to express himself deeply with his own body ... precisely through the 'sincere gift' of self." It is "in his body as man or woman [that] man feels he is a subject of holiness" (TOB 19:5). Indeed, a holy fascination with our bodies as male and female is *precisely the key* that opens the holy door to the divine bridal chamber, allowing us to experience what the mystics call "nuptial union" with God. This deep, intimate, transforming union with God imbues us with authentic holiness.

This is the "word" that we must come to "read" in our bodies. In fact, this Word of divine love has, itself, *become flesh*. Sadly, like the disciples on the road to Emmaus, we are often kept from recognizing this Word. We see the body with our eyes, but our blinded spirits fail to recognize the "great mystery" of Christ. But listen to these glorious words of hope from Pope Benedict XVI: "At the breaking of the bread [the disciples with whom Christ walked to Emmaus] experience in reverse fashion what happened to Adam and Eve when they ate the fruit of the tree of the knowledge of good and evil: their eyes are opened" (SL, p. 121). Adam and Eve lost sight of the "great mystery" revealed through their bodies; through the breaking of the bread – the infinite grace of the Eucharist – we can regain it! As we allow this grace continually to have its way in us, purifying our hearts ever more fully, we come to see and experience that our creation as male and female and our call to become one-flesh is a "great mystery" that points us to Christ and the Church (see Eph 5:31-32). In fact, as John Paul wrote, "The Church cannot be understood ... unless we keep in mind the 'great mystery' involved in the creation of man as male and female and the vocation of both to conjugal love, to fatherhood and to motherhood" (LF 19).

Holy fascination with the body and with God's plan for sexual union unleashes love. And love, John Paul tells us, *"unleashes a special experience of the beautiful,* which focuses on what is visible, although at the same time it involves the entire person" (TOB 108:6). An integrated understanding of beauty always involves the whole person. The lover exults: "Behold, you are beautiful, my love, behold, you are beautiful! Your eyes are doves behind your veil. Your hair is like a flock of goats moving down the slopes of Gilead" (Song 4:1).

The Pope acknowledges that such metaphors of beauty might surprise us today. (I can't quite imagine my wife being flattered if I compared her hair to a flock of goats.) Even if the imagery sounds odd to modern ears, the metaphors of the Song "as well as the very force with which they are expressed" have kept their value (TOB 109:1). And they show us how the "language" of the body as male and female seeks support and confirmation in the whole visible world (see TOB 108:8). The beauty of the human sexual-body-person is the pinnacle of all created beauty in the visible world. And the lovers of the Song find themselves appealing to the beauty of the visible world to express what they see in each other. Yet, in the end, metaphors fall short. Leaving them behind, the bridegroom says, "You are all beautiful, my beloved, and there is no blemish in you" (4:7). And further on, beckoning her to "open" to him, he calls her "my perfect one" (5:2).

Yearning for Perfect Beauty

John Paul tells us that the bridegroom's desire is "a search for integral beauty, for purity free from every stain; it is a search for perfection that contains ... *the synthesis of human beauty, beauty of soul and body*" (TOB 112:3). The longing of the lover for "pure beauty" is both an echo of "the beginning" and a premonition of the future. In the beginning, before sin, the naked human body perfectly reflected the beauty of God. That beauty was lost because of the "blemish" and "stain" of original sin. But at the end of time, the bodies of all who respond to the divine marriage proposal will be raised to a level of participation in God's beauty beyond even that of the beginning. The lover of the Song *yearns* for this, as do we all.

The modern cult-of-the-all-perfect-body, with its endless rituals and "sacraments," is really a substitute for a living faith in the resurrection of our bodies. We are constantly fighting the inevitable prospect of death and decay, not with faith in Christ and his resurrection, but with faith in Oil-of-Olay™ and cosmetic surgery. The modern world has substituted the fading and fabricated "beauty" of a facelift for the unfading and fabulous beauty of a "grace lift."

In the Song of Songs, the "spotless" beauty of the body points to the "spotless" beauty of the soul, to the beauty and radiance of true holiness. Holiness *is* beautiful, and beauty *is* holy – for true beauty is always a gift of God. As the Pope states, love actually *obliges* the husband to desire his bride's beauty, to cherish it and care for it. Even more, the husband, through his own sacrificial love, is called in some way to uncover, discover, foster, even "create" his bride's beauty, desiring all that is good for her. The husband's ability to see and foster his wife's beauty is, in fact, a test and measure of his love (see TOB 92:4). For the husband is to love his wife *as Christ loved the church*. And Christ "gave himself up for her ... that he might present the church to himself in splendor, without spot or wrinkle or any such thing, that she might be holy and without blemish" (Eph 5:25-27). Husbands would do well to ask themselves: *Where does my wife doubt her own beauty? Where is she unaware of her own beauty?* It is precisely *there* that the husband must love her most tenderly and, through that love, help awaken in her the realization of her own beauty.

In the Marriage of the Lamb, when we are all fully "awakened" to our beauty, we will discover the true, integral beauty of everyone who forms the great communion of saints. It will be a beauty "free from every stain," a *"beauty of soul and body,"* as John Paul says. And this dazzling beauty of every human being will be but a dim reflection, a little glimmer of the beauty of the Eternal One whom we will behold "face to face."

"Eyes of the Body" and "Eyes of the Heart"

Integral beauty is seen both with the "eyes of the body" and the "eyes of the heart." Both the bridegroom and the bride in the Song see with this integral vision, although each with a different emphasis. As John Paul observes, the man seems to see his beloved's attractiveness more with the "eyes of the body" while the woman's affection is aroused more by the "eyes of the heart." As experience attests, men tend to be more visual in their appreciation of beauty and women tend to be more "interior."

Obviously, this doesn't mean men don't appreciate interior beauty and women don't appreciate physical beauty. But the dispositions of men and women tend to differ. In the Song, the visible expression of femininity seems to prevail in the bridegroom's words, whereas for the bride, their physical closeness causes "the *growth* of the intimate '*language of the heart*'" (TOB 111:2). Each disposition, however, finds balance in the other. And both dispositions, properly integrated, lead to wonder and amazement at the mystery of the other as a sexual-body-person and to wonder and amazement at the *love* through which the mystery of the other is revealed (see TOB 109:1). And it is "a love filled with pleasure" (TOB 108:8).

The value and dignity of the other in the enchanting mystery of sexual difference shines over *everything* in their relationship (see TOB 109:2). This, in turn, helps us to understand who the man *is* for the woman and who she *is* for him. They are not merely sexual objects for each other, but sexual *subjects* – they are sexual *persons* reflecting a divine mystery towards which each is filled with awe and wonder. And this awe and wonder, John Paul tells us, is nothing other than a spiritually mature experience of sexual attraction (see TOB 117b:4).

Authentic sexual attraction is always an attraction to the beauty of the other *as a person*, not merely as an object of selfish consumption. This is the enormous value of the virtue of chastity. To summarize what John Paul II wrote in his pre-papal book *Love and Responsibility*, the essence of chastity consists in quickness to affirm the value of the person in every situation, and in raising to the personal level all reactions to a person's body and sex. It is not a matter of "annihilating" sexual reactions or pushing them into the subconscious where they await an opportunity to explode. Chastity is rather a matter of sustained long-term integration of sexual values with the value of the person (see LR, 170-171). For example, if I am walking through an airport and am tempted to lust after a woman walking by, I shouldn't respond by seeking to annihilate or delete my attraction to this woman. Rather, I should seek interiorly to integrate her sexual values (that which I found myself attracted to) with her true dignity as a person. With a humble trust in God's desire to heal my lustful, disintegrated heart, I might pray: *Lord, thank you for the beauty of this person. She is made in your image and likeness and is never to be looked upon as an object for my gratification. Help me to see the mystery of your beauty revealed through her beauty. Amen.*

Each lover in the Song sees the value and dignity of the other person not despite his or her sexual values, but *precisely in and through them*: "His lips are lilies ... his body is ivory ... his legs are alabaster columns" (6:13-15). "Your breasts are like two fawns, twins of a gazelle. Your neck is like an ivory tower" (7:3). Such recognition of the value of the person *in and through that person's sexual values* (this is what sexual integration entails) is absolutely critical if men and women are to become a true sign of divine love when they unite in "one flesh." Otherwise, a sexual union may take place, but, because of a lack of integration, it doesn't correspond to the true dignity of the persons involved.

Failure in sexual integration – that is, a failure to recognize the true dignity of the person in and through his or her sexual values – leads in one of two directions. It leads towards an *angelistic* rejection of sexual values in favor of a dis-embodied version of the human person (as if that were possible), or an *animalistic* indulgence in those sexual values divorced from the true dignity of the person. As Pope Benedict XVI states, "Man is truly himself [only] when his body and soul are intimately united; the challenge of *eros* can be said to be truly overcome when this unification is achieved" (DC 5).

How is this unification achieved? It is a long and exacting work, to be sure. It is precisely the lifelong journey of the interior life spoken of in the Prologue. John Paul provides a window into what this journey looks like in the following lengthy passage, which I paraphrase: We must learn with perseverance and consistency the meaning of our bodies, the meaning of our sexuality. We must learn this not only in the abstract (although that, too, is necessary), but above all in the interior reactions of our own "hearts." This is a "science," the Pope says, which cannot really be learned only from books, because it is a question here of deep knowledge of our interior life. Deep in the heart we learn to distinguish between what, on the one hand, composes the great riches of sexuality and sexual attraction, and what, on the other hand, bears only the sign of lust. And although these internal movements of the heart can sometimes be confused with each other, we have been *called by Christ to acquire a mature and complete evaluation allowing us to distinguish and judge the various movements of our hearts.* Then John Paul concludes: "One should add that this task *can* be carried out and that it is truly worthy of man" (TOB 48:4).

The men's group at Bill's parish has been doing a guided study of John Paul II's TOB for several months. It has helped him tremendously to understand why, in his fallen humanity, he has found pornography so attractive. "I have hungered, and I mean hungered, for woman's beauty my whole life. I can remember that curiosity from a very young age. But porn warped my understanding of what a woman's beauty is. I became fixated on physical perfection. And what's that line of the Pope? He says something about the man in the Song of Songs longing for perfect beauty. Yes! Yes! I can relate. But I guess I've been fixated on a very superficial understanding of beauty."

One of the great epiphanies for the men in Bill's group has been realizing that being a Christian does not mean repressing sexual desire, but allowing it to be transformed. "I'd been to so many priests, and so many men's groups over the years. They either seemed to imply that my lusts were normal and it was no big deal, or they gave me the impression that this deep hunger for feminine beauty in me was evil and I needed to squash it. It seems every guy struggles with this. We go from one extreme to the next and keep beating ourselves up. Here [in John Paul II's TOB] there's a balance. A call to redemption, like I can actually reclaim something of that vision of beauty that Adam had of Eve in the garden. For cryin' out loud, that's what I've been looking for the whole time! The more I enter into this, the more I catch glimpses of my wife's true beauty. But, man!, it's a battle."

Bill knows he has a long way to go to experience that spiritually mature form of sexual attraction that John Paul writes about. His struggle with porn isn't over. He's thinking of joining a twelve-step group for sexual addiction. He recently moved his computer into the living room and has taken other precautions to avoid what he calls a "steady flow" of temptation. Bad habits die hard. But he is committed to the journey. "I want to see my wife's true beauty so bad! I want to love her in the right way! I'm seeing more clearly now why my issues have caused Linda so much pain. And it grieves me."

Reflection Questions

I. Our culture constantly bombards us with images of what it considers "ideal physical beauty." How have these images affected my own ideas about beauty? How have these images affected my sense of my own beauty?

2. St. Peter says that a woman's beauty should not come from outward adornment, from concern with hairstyles and jewelry and clothing. All of that fades. Instead, a woman's beauty should come from within, from "the hidden person of the heart." Such beauty is unfading (see I Pt 3:3-4).

> *Men:* Is this the kind of beauty I am attracted to? If not, why not?
> *Women:* Is this the kind of beauty I strive for? If not, why not?

3. Perhaps you are familiar with Dostoevsky's statement, "I believe in the end the world will be saved by beauty." What do you think he means? Do you think he is correct?

Suggested Prayer

Jesus, your masculinity perfectly reflects the Beauty of God.

Mary, your femininity perfectly reflects the Beauty of God.

Beauty of Jesus, heal all diseased images and ideas I have of the masculine body.

Beauty of Mary, heal all the diseased images and ideas I have of the feminine body.

Heavenly Father, have mercy on me, a sinner. I want to see! I want to see your Beauty reflected in all you have created and one day to see your Uncreated Beauty face to face. Amen.

Chapter 3

"My Sister, My Bride"

Diane heard a knock on her door. She didn't know how her life was about to change, but she knew his name was Larry. One of her friends had set her up with him in hopes that it would "get her over" a recent, painful break-up. Diane admits that she never really liked the idea of a blind date. She had always dreamed as a girl that she would marry a boy who was her *friend* before he was her *boyfriend*. The expectation of immediate romance just didn't seem natural. But this was the college scene in the late 1980s, and the rampant promiscuity of dorm life had forced her to relinquish her "naive" girlhood expectations. If she wanted a man in her life, she had to conform to the scene. Or so she thought.

"I even remember hoping that night that he would want to make-out with me. If a guy didn't want to make out with you, it was considered an insult." Larry wanted to ... and more. Diane reluctantly lost her virginity to Larry about six months later and married him about three years after that. Fourteen years and three kids later, she moved out.

It is essential, as John Paul says, for men and women to know who they "are" for each other (see TOB 109:3) – that is, who and what God made man and woman *to be* for each other. This is essential not only for the health of the marital relationship. This is also vitally important for life and society in general. For, according to John Paul II, the dignity and balance of human life depend at every moment of history and at every point on the globe on who woman will be for man and who man will be for woman (see TOB 43:7). The sexual relationship – the relationship of man to woman and woman to man – is the deepest foundation of human ethics and culture (see TOB 45:3). The union of man and woman builds and shapes families, families shape neighborhoods, neighborhoods shape communities, communities shape cities, cities shape states, states shape nations, nations shape the world. When the sexual relationship breaks down, eventually so does everything resting on it.

What is the sexual relationship supposed to be? How is it to take shape in a way that leads to human flourishing rather than breakdown? John Paul focuses on two themes from the Song of Songs which shine a bright light on this question. The first could be called the "fraternal" theme (see TOB 110:5), and the second the theme of "inviolability" (see TOB 110:8). We will look at the former in this chapter and the latter in the next.

The Bride Is First a Sister

Several times throughout the Song, the lover refers to his bride first as his sister. "You have ravished my heart, my sister, my bride, you have ravished my heart with one glance of your eyes ... How sweet is your love, my sister, my bride!" (4:9–10) According to John Paul, these expressions say much more than if he had called her by her actual name. They illustrate how love reveals the other person. "The fact that in this approach the feminine 'I' is revealed for the bridegroom as 'sister' — and that *she is bride* precisely *as sister* — has a particular eloquence" (TOB 109:4). The lover's words are "impregnated with a particular content" (TOB 110:1). They reveal that he sees her not as a thing to be appropriated, but as a *person* to be loved. To be a person "means both 'being subject,' but also 'being in relation'" (TOB 109:4). The term "sister" denotes this. It speaks of the two different ways in which masculinity and femininity "incarnate" the same humanity, and it speaks of their being in reciprocal relationship.

Obviously, the term "sister" also allows the man to be understood as brother. "O that you were like a brother to me, that nursed at my mother's breast!" (8:1). John Paul observes that recognizing each other as brother and sister presents a certain *challenge* for the man (see TOB 109:4). It challenges him to assess his motives. Is he motivated by love or by lust, by the sincere gift of self or merely by a desire to gratify himself? The bridegroom of the Song accepts this challenge and gives a spontaneous answer to it (see TOB 109:4): "Do not stir up nor awaken love until it please [before she wants it!]" (8:4). And further on he says, "We have a little sister, and she has no breasts. What shall we do for our sister, on the day when she is spoken for?" (8:8). These verses are sufficient proof, according to John Paul, that the bridegroom accepts the challenge of being a "brother" to her and of recognizing her as "sister."

As the Pope poignantly expresses, the "bridegroom's words tend to reproduce ... the history of the femininity of the beloved person; they see her still in the time of girlhood ('We have a little sister, and she still has no breasts')." In this way, the bridegroom's words "embrace her entire 'I,' soul and body, *with a disinterested tenderness*" (TOB 110:2). This doesn't mean the lover is not *interested* in his beloved. He is deeply interested in her, but not selfishly so. He is not out to "get" something selfishly for himself. He wants to love her tenderly, for her own sake. In turn, he takes great delight in the sweetness of her love for him as something "much better than wine" (4:10). But his specific focus is on her, on what is good for *her*, not on what is in it for *him*.

The same "disinterested tenderness" carries through when the term "sister" gives way to the term "bride." The transition from "sister" to "bride" maintains — and it must maintain — the same recognition of her personhood, of her dignity as "sister." This is the special eloquence of calling her "sister" *before* calling her "bride." It reveals that the lover's mode of operation in desiring her as bride is love, not lust. And love forms "a reciprocal relation ... through marriage similar to the one that unites brother and sister." In fact, "through marriage man and woman become brother and sister in a special way" (TOB 114:3). They become brother and sister in a way that is actually rooted in authentic spousal love. "This is the reason," as the Pope states, "for *the convergence (and not divergence) of both expressions*" (TOB 109:6).

Common Belonging Brings Peace

The "fraternal theme" speaks of their common humanity and a shared sense of belonging. As John Paul says rather poetically, it is as if "they descended from the same family circle, as though from infancy they had been united by memories of the common hearth. In this way, they reciprocally feel as close as brother and sister who owe their existence to the same mother" (TOB 110:1).

As the Pope said in his reflections on Genesis: "Before they become husband and wife ... man and woman *come forth from the mystery of creation* first of all *as brother and sister in the same humanity*" (TOB 18:5).

The first man and woman had a "sense of belonging to the Creator as their common Father." This experience of common belonging – of being "brother-sister" in the same humanity – provided the foundation of their unity as spouses in "one flesh" (Gen 2:24). Becoming "one flesh" refers not only to the joining of two bodies but is a "'sacramental' expression which corresponds to the communion of persons" (TOB 31:2). Only persons can enter "communion," that common-union in which – through a free, sincere, and reciprocal gift of self – persons enter into a mutually affirming and life-giving relationship. Such a relationship is based not on instinct, but on love – freely given, freely received, freely returned, and freely received in return.

These same themes from Genesis are "wonderfully developed in the Song of Songs" (TOB 110:3). Here John Paul specifically reminds us that the goal of his reflections on the erotic poetry of the Song is to understand marital love as a "sign" communicating divine life/grace (see TOB 110:3). This sign is constituted and divine grace communicated in so far as spouses reread the "language of the body" according to the truth of God's intention for man and woman as outlined in Genesis. The lovers in the Song successfully reread the original "language" that God inscribed in their bodies and speak it – or, rather, *sing* it – to each other truthfully, in splendid harmony.

It is precisely this peaceful harmony that allows them to live their mutual closeness in security and to manifest it without fearing the unfair judgment of others. They are not ashamed of their love because they are confident in its purity. As the beloved says, "If I met you outside, I would kiss you, and none would despise me" (8:41). From this experience a deep inner tranquility arises, reminiscent of

that profound peace in each other's presence that allowed the first man
and woman to be "naked without shame" (Gen 2:25).

Why do we feel the need to cover our bodies (specifically our sexual
values) in a fallen world? We cover our bodies in a fallen world not because
they are "bad." The notion that our bodies are bad is a heresy! We cover our
bodies in a fallen world because they are *so good* and we feel an instinctive
need to protect the goodness of the body from the degradation of lust.
In the beginning, before sin, man and woman did not experience shame
precisely because they did not experience lust. *This does not mean they did not
experience sexual desire.* Rather, it means their erotic desire was not tainted by
selfishness. The "fire" of their desire was one of pure self-donating love,
and pure self-donating love is the sign of true holiness! This is why they
were naked without shame – because they were holy (see TOB 19:5). They
were swimming in an ocean of divine love. And, as we can observe, there
is no need for a bathing suit in this ocean.

The lovers of the Song are swimming in the same ocean of divine
love. "So I was in his eyes as one who finds peace" (8:10). While this
is a peace found deep in the human heart, nonetheless John Paul says
it is also a "peace of the body." Above all, John Paul describes it as *the
peace of the encounter* of man and woman as the image of God *by means of
a reciprocal and disinterested gift of self* (see TOB 110:2).

This is the richness and the challenge of the words "my sister,
my bride." It challenges both the man and the woman to find in their
union a true, luminous "image of God." For, with the help of both
Genesis and the Song of Songs, we "can deduce that *man became the
image of God not only through his own humanity, but also through the communion
of persons,* which man and woman form from the very beginning. The
function of the image is that of mirroring the one who is the model,

of reproducing its own prototype" (TOB 9:3). The prototype, God himself, does not exist in eternal solitude, but in eternal *communion* – an eternal Communion of three divine Persons. Thus, the human being "becomes an image of God not so much in the moment of solitude as in the moment of communion" – a communion that is not closed in on itself, but rather a communion upon which "right from the beginning, the blessing of fruitfulness descended." And, according to John Paul, this great mystery of our call to image God in fruitful communion "constitutes, perhaps, the deepest theological aspect of everything one can say about man" (TOB 9:3).

Lust Is Blind to the "Sister-Bride"

Recognizing the "brother-sister theme" within the language of sexuality is critical in order to understand properly who woman truly *is* for man and who man truly *is* for woman. It demonstrates clearly that the true language of sexuality cannot be determined by biological urges alone. Left to itself in this fallen world, the mere sexual urge would not recognize the woman as "sister." And for lack of such recognition, it could not recognize her properly as "bride." She would be for him only an object of appropriation – that is, an object to be grasped, possessed, used.

The lovers of the Song bear witness precisely to the fact that authentic eros is not aimed at appropriation and selfish satisfaction. Rather, true eros expresses itself "in the reciprocal ecstasy," John Paul says, "of the good and the beautiful in love ... The terms 'my sister, my bride' seem to arise precisely from this deep level and only on the basis of that level can they be interpreted adequately" (TOB 110:4). The fraternal theme does not dampen eros as some might imagine. Rather, it heightens it by giving eros a solid launching pad from which to ascend towards the true, good, and beautiful – and, beyond that, towards ultimate Truth, Goodness, and Beauty itself (God).

Interestingly, I have observed differing reactions from men and women when I have presented the "sister-bride" concept in the classroom and at seminars. For whatever reason, most women respond readily, as if such an idea confirms their deepest hopes for a relationship. You can almost see it on their faces – "Gosh, I wish the men I knew would treat me first as a *sister*." Men, on the other hand, often seem taken aback. To consider a potential "sex partner" as a "sister" cuts right at the heart of what men tend to desire in a relationship. The look on many men's faces seems to say, "*Sister?* C'mon! You don't do *that* with a sister." This is precisely the point! A man revolts at the idea of indulging lust with his "sister" – and so should he revolt at the thought of indulging lust with his bride.

Aren't brothers usually the first to defend their sisters from the lusts of men? Think of the older brother who gets *very* protective when his developing sister starts attracting the attention of boys at school. When a man recognizes his beloved as sister, that same brotherly instinct impels him to protect her from the lusts of men – including, and especially, his own lusts.

Marriage is *not* a legitimate outlet for one's lusts. As the Pope states clearly, "A man can commit ... adultery 'in the heart' even with his own wife, if he treats her only as an object for the satisfaction of instinct" (TOB 43:3). The same, of course, could be said of a woman towards her husband. Women know how to use and manipulate men just as much as men know how to use and manipulate women. We must acknowledge this clearly: both the male and the female personality are capable of lust, and the lustful distortions of each cut the other like a knife. And marriage *never* makes this "cutting" of lust "okay." When John Paul made this point, a firestorm of criticism erupted in the international media accusing the Pope of condemning sex *even in marriage*. One critic retorted, "If a man can't lust after his wife, then whom *can* he lust after?" Uh, that would be *no one*. Lust is always wrong. But it didn't even register on this guy's radar that there is *another way to see, another way to think, another way to experience* sexual desire and union. Indulging lust or repressing it are not the only two options.

The lovers of the Song could hardly be accused of repressing their desires: "Let my beloved come to his garden, and eat its choicest fruits. I come to my garden, my sister, my bride, I gather my myrrh with my spice, I eat my honeycomb with my honey ... My beloved put his hand to the latch, and my heart was thrilled within me" (4:16-5:1, 4). But nor is this a base indulgence of lust. Rather, the lovers of the Song are somehow experiencing *another dimension of eros* — an eros that has launched beyond the stifling bonds of lust's gravitational pull and into the weightless freedom of an intoxication of love that knows no limits.

As the Flemish mystic Blessed John van Ruysbroeck beautifully expressed it: "In its ascent, love, without losing order, loses measure and finds intoxication" (cited in CL, p. 81). Love yearns to abandon itself, to let loose, to free itself from all restraint and measure, to drink all the wine she desires (recall Teresa of Avila's comment). But this kind of holy-abandoned-intoxication lies on the *other side* of lust's gravitational pull, and the passover into zero-gravity can be excruciating. Few are willing to endure those "g's." It is called "crucifixion with Christ." Only if we are willing to "die with Christ" can we also expect to enter the ecstasies of his resurrection. Lust must be placed on the altar of sacrifice, not with the goal of annihilating human desire, but with the surety of faith that the satisfaction of eros can be found only by passing over into the eternal nuptial-fire-love-bomb-explosion of agape.

Lacking such faith, we usually lean in one of two directions: we may attempt to shut down our desires altogether (repression), or abandon ourselves to desire on *this side* of lust's gravitational pull (indulgence). When the former happens, a person leans towards puritanism. Repression may masquerade as virtue, but it really points to the presence of vice. When the latter happens, love, in its failure to lose measure, loses order. All hell breaks lose. Lustful passions reign. Persons are turned into consumer objects for the satisfaction of base instincts. And our deepest desires for infinite love lie shipwrecked on the finite shores that promised fulfillment but couldn't possibly deliver.

Recognizing each other as brother and sister *before* recognizing each other as "sexual partner," as husband and wife, is the key to experiencing something of heaven rather than something of hell in the sexual relationship. It compels us to face the distortions of lust and to seek grace in "untwisting" those distortions. Only as sexual desire is reoriented towards infinite love can it lose measure without losing order.

Diane has been living on her own for about six months, but she and Larry are still trying to save their marriage. Some friends recommended they contact The Alexander House – a ministry that offers "marriage coaching" based on John Paul II's TOB. They meet by phone once a week with a mentor couple who has been helping them examine their relationship in light of God's original plan for man and woman and the redemption Christ offers us.

One of the issues that came out early on in their coaching sessions was a deep bitterness and resentment that Diane carries in her heart towards Larry. Reading John Paul's teaching about the "fraternal theme" of love helped her understand why. Years of pent-up anger exploded during one of their phone meetings with their coaching couple: "You didn't really love me! From the very first night I met you, you just wanted to get up my shirt!"

Mercy and forgiveness is a constant theme of these coaching sessions. But Diane has learned that this does *not* mean sweeping the pain under the rug or trying to forget how Larry has wounded her. As an "assignment" between sessions, the coaching couple asked Diane to spend some time reflecting on this passage from the *Catechism*: "It is not in our power not to feel or to forget an offense; but the heart that offers itself to the Holy Spirit turns injury into compassion and purifies the memory in transforming the hurt into intercession" (CCC 2843). As Diane is beginning to see, when we offer our pain to God, it becomes redemptive, not only for the person pained, but also – and this is the real miracle of mercy – *for the person who caused the pain in the first place*. Beyond the pain Larry has caused her, Diane has also had to face ways in which she had wounded *herself* by not being true to herself and by allowing her own lusts – lusts for attention, approval, acceptance, security, etc. – to play a role in how their relationship unfolded.

Larry's "assignment" was different. First, the coaching couple asked him to consider ways Diane had wounded him and to allow any anger about that to surface – not to be dumped on Diane, but to be given to Christ. "Jesus," they said, "can transform your anger into mercy and compassion, if you let him." Releasing Diane to God's mercy would free him, his coaches told him, to be more sincere in the second part of his assignment. He was to think of a way in which he could begin to make amends for the pain he had caused Diane. He acknowledged to Diane how their relationship had started on the wrong foot and asked her if she would be willing to go out on their "first date" all over again. He said he wanted to get to know her as a friend and as a sister and he assured her that he would be a gentleman. So, the other night, like seventeen years before, Diane heard a knock at her door. She didn't know how her life was about to change, but she knew his name was Larry.

Reflection Questions

I. Have I been in relationships that skipped the "fraternal theme" and jumped immediately into romance and/or sexual activity? If so, what effect did that have on me and on the other person in the relationship?

2. If the terms "sister" and "bride" ("brother" and "husband") seem to be in conflict, reflect on the reason for that. Where, along the way of my own formation, did I come to believe that being "brother and sister" to each other was incompatible with being passionate lovers? What personal ideas or attitudes

might I need to address in order to recognize the compatibility of the terms "sister" and "bride"?

Suggested Prayer

Jesus, you are the fully restored Adam, and through your death and resurrection, you fully restored Eve. Show me the path of restoration. Show me the path of sexual redemption, of true sexual liberation from all that keeps me bound. By the power of your death and resurrection, untwist in me what sin has twisted so that I might experience sexual desire as you created it to be, as the desire to love in your image. Amen.

Chapter 4

"A Garden Closed, A Fountain Sealed"

The evidence had been mounting, and Kathy could not hide the truth when her husband finally confronted her: "Are you having an affair?"

A few days later, she sent me an email seeking advice. In my response, I suggested, among many other things, that she turn to the Blessed Mother in her pain. She singled out this line from my email and shot back: "Are you crazy? I can't talk to her about this. She's too holy. She's the Blessed Virgin – and I'm anything but."

With the help of the Song of Songs, we have been exploring who man and woman "are" for each other according to God's original plan, why God gave man and woman to each other and how to live in accord with that. In Chapter 3 we looked at the "fraternal" theme as the foundation of the sexual relationship. Now we will look at the theme of "inviolability."

Entering the Mystery

There is something awe-inspiring about each and every human being. We all have a particular and unique richness, an inner life, an inner self, something spiritual that even the most advanced animals do not possess. To recognize the "inviolability" of a person is to recognize the unique inner mystery of that person and to commit oneself to honoring it. Authentic love, as John Paul tells us, allows a kind of "entering" into the mystery of the person without ever violating the mystery of the person (see TOB 111:1). If a person's "love" violates the one loved, if it attacks the person's true dignity, then *it is not love* and should not be called love. It is one of love's many counterfeits — lust usually being first among them.

We discover the theme of "inviolability" in the following passage of the Song of Songs: "A garden locked is my sister, my bride, a garden closed, a fountain sealed" (4:12). These metaphors, according to John Paul, both confirm and surpass what was expressed by the name "sister," revealing another vision of the feminine mystery. The Pope sees in the poetic riches of these images "not only a beauty of language, but a beauty of the truth expressed by this language" (TOB 110:6). As we seek to enter the truth expressed by this language, it would be wise to "take off our shoes," for this is holy ground. Indeed, if we follow John Paul into the depth of this mystery we will find ourselves "behind the veil," having mystically entered the innermost sanctuary of God's dwelling place — the "holy of holies." This is also the most delicate material of the Pope's catechesis. In light of what follows, one can understand why John Paul concluded that an abridged version would be more appropriate for the young ears present at his Wednesday addresses.

The Personal Mystery of Femininity

The metaphors "garden closed" and "fountain sealed" remain in a very strict relation with sexual intercourse and, thus, help us to understand its mystery, especially the mystery of "the woman," who must trustingly open to receive her bridegroom (see TOB 110:7). John Paul observes that in the design of God right "from the beginning," femininity actually determines the mystery of sexual union. The feminine body-person "says more" or "reveals more" about the meaning of becoming one-flesh. With the metaphors of the garden and fountain, we find ourselves in the "vestibule" of that union (see TOB 110:8) – just on the verge of entering into its mystery.

We can see the great value of these expressions, the Pope says, in their ability to convey the profoundly personal dimension and meaning of the union of the lovers. "The language of metaphors – poetic language – seems to be especially appropriate and precise in this sphere" (TOB 110:8). Both of these metaphors – "garden closed" and "fountain sealed" – express the whole *personal dignity of the female sex*. They speak with profound reverence of the mystery of the feminine body – of "what seems most profoundly hidden" in God's mysterious design of woman (see TOB 110:7).

But why is the garden "closed" and the fountain "sealed"? John Paul says that this indicates the woman's "personal structure of self-possession" (TOB 110:7). In the very structure of her sexual mystery, the woman holds the key to her own "garden," which remains closed until she – and she alone – wills to open it. She is in total possession of herself and stands before her lover as such. As John Paul poignantly expresses it, "The bride *presents herself to the eyes of the man as the master of her own mystery*" (TOB 110:7).

Recognizing this, the lover knows he cannot "take" her or "grasp" her. He, of course, *longs* with all his being to enter her mystery, her garden. For, as St. Louis de Montfort states, commenting on the "enclosed garden" of the Song, "There are in this earthly paradise untold riches, beauties, rarities, and delights ... There are flowerbeds ... diffusing a fragrance which delights even the angels" (TD 261). Here de Montfort is referring specifically to Mary, whom the Church, in both her liturgy and theological tradition, recognizes as the embodiment of the bride in the Song of Songs. However, in-as-much as every woman shares in Mary's dignity, de Montfort's comment can be extended to every bride. In short, the bridegroom is intoxicated with his bride's fragrance. The fragrance of her garden is like "henna with nard, nard and saffron, calamus and cinnamon ... myrrh and aloes, with all chief spices" (4:13-14). For she has opened her petals "like a rose growing by a stream of water," sending forth "fragrance like frankincense" (Sir 39:13-14). How could this glorious aroma not awaken the lover's desire? But, the lover knows that if he is to respect woman as "master of her own mystery," he must submit his yearning to her, entrusting himself to her as a gift, placing himself entirely at her mercy — awaiting *and respecting* her response.

If the man were to barge into this "closed garden" (in thought or deed), or if he were to manipulate her into surrendering the key, he would not be loving her, he would be violating her, using her, asserting himself as master over her. And persons, precisely as persons, must never be mastered. It is an intrinsic violation of human dignity. This is not so for dogs, horses, or elephants. Of course, we hope Dumbo's master isn't cruel, but simply to place oneself as master over an animal is not a violation of that animal, whereas it is for a person.

Why? Because, as persons, we are our own agents, the masters of our own decisions. No one can substitute his act of will for mine without encroaching on and violating my turf. This is what John Paul means by the "inviolability" of the person. Philosophers also call this the "incommunicable" aspect of personhood — that which cannot be given, communicated, or surrendered to another. Someone might very much want me to want what he wants, but no one can want *for* me, and no one can force me to want what he wants. This is where the impassible limit between persons, dictated by free will, becomes clear. "I am, and must be, independent in my actions. All human relationships are posited on this fact. All true conceptions about education and culture begin from and return to this point" (LR, p. 24).

In the sexual sphere, it often happens that a man, for instance, wants a woman to want what he wants (it can go the other way too, of course). What will he do if she herself does not want what he wants? Here the man stands at the critical impasse of persons, a critical fork in the road. One prong leads to love and the other to its antithesis — to domination and use. Which will it be? The man must exercise his freedom as a person and choose. I have spoken to many a man who has admitted to subtle and not so subtle forms of manipulation in this regard. I, myself, have faced this fork and chosen the wrong prong. "What becomes apparent," the Pope says, "in this dynamic of love, is *the impossibility, as it were, of one person being appropriated and mastered by the other. The person is someone who stands above all* [measures] *of appropriation and domination, of possession and satisfaction*" (TOB 113:3).

The Closed Garden Opens ...

The language of the body reread truthfully keeps pace with *the discovery of the inner inviolability of the person* (see TOB 110:8). In other words, sexual love as it was meant to be always respects the mystery of the beloved and refuses utterly to violate that mystery. The lover's declaration of his beloved as a "closed garden" and a "sealed fountain" attests to the sincerity of his own gift of self. He is knocking at the door, not breaking in. He is loving her, not dominating her. He is initiating the gift of himself and awaiting her response, not asserting his will over, above, and regardless of hers.

With deep longing, the lover makes his desire clear: "Open to me, my sister, my love, my dove, my perfect one; for my head is wet with dew" (5:2). And she hears him: "Listen, my beloved is knocking" (5:2). But, respecting her fully as "master of her own mystery," he puts "his hand to the latch" (5:4) only with her freely given "yes" — a yes given without any hint of being coerced or manipulated. The bride knows that the bridegroom's longing is *for her* — for her whole feminine body-soul mystery, not merely a reductive desire for her body — so she goes confidently to meet him with the gift of herself. In total freedom, she surrenders to him; she "opens her garden" to him, making it *his*:

> Awake, O north wind, and come, O south wind!
> Blow upon my garden, let its fragrance be wafted abroad.
> Let my beloved come to his garden, and eat its choicest fruits. (4:16)

> I had put off my garment ...
> My beloved put his hand to the latch, and my heart was thrilled
> > within me.
> I arose to open to my beloved, and my hands dripped with
> > myrrh,
> my fingers with liquid myrrh, upon the handles of the bolt.
> I opened to my beloved ... (5:3-6)

> My beloved has gone down to his garden, to the beds of spices,
> > to pasture his flock in the gardens, and to gather the lilies.
> I am my beloved's and my beloved is mine;

He pastures his flock among the lilies. (6:2-3)

These boldly erotic verses overflow with a fragrant and sacred sensuality. Far from glorifying lust, John Paul insists that these verses reveal the power of "authentic love" (TOB 110:9). In these verses we see how *"the 'garden closed' opens up in some way before the eyes of the bridegroom's soul and body"* (TOB 111:4). And with profound reverence and awe he beholds her mystery unveiled – that mystery of which she remains the master. Her openness is offered with the full freedom of her own choice, in the full freedom of the gift. She, and she alone, is able to unveil her mystery, and the bridegroom of the Song is fully aware of this. He refuses to extort her gift.

As she opens to him, he approaches her with tenderness, ever desiring to ensure her that her trust of him is not in vain. He comes to her delighting in her gift, remaining ever in awe of her freely opened garden: "I come to my garden, my sister, my bride, I gather my myrrh with my spice, I eat my honeycomb with my honey, I drink my wine with my milk" (5:1). *Oh the delight of satisfying this holy desire!* And that is what the lovers of the Song are expressing – *holy* desire.

As John Paul says, "The presence of these elements in this book that enters into the canon of Sacred Scripture shows that they ... contain a primordial and essential sign of holiness" (TOB 109:2). If we are to enter through this *gateway to holiness* opened to us by the Song of Songs, all suspicion towards the body must be abandoned at the threshold; all depreciations of sexuality – be they of the prudish or base kind – must be submitted to the glorious Truth of this simultaneously sacred and unabashedly sexual Song; and all fear of our own desires surrendered to the purifying fire of the Mystery. The suffering we must bear, the crucifixion we must endure to passover into "the love without measure," is well worth it. For through this gateway, as John Paul tell us — and here we are speaking of the allegorical meaning of the Song — lies "the ineffable joy experienced by the mystics as 'nuptial union'" (NMI 33) — "nuptial union," that is, *with God himself*.

Entering the Mystery

John Paul II's TOB, deeply rooted in the spousal mysticism of St. John of the Cross, provides the key to the wine cellar spoken of in the Song of Songs: "The king has brought me into his wine cellar" (Song 1:4). In other words, understanding the theological mystery of our own sexual bodies and their summons to become "one flesh" is the key that opens us to the ineffable joy of "nuptial union" with God. For the union of the sexes "is a great mystery and it refers to Christ and the church" (Eph 5:32).

This means, as mentioned in the Introduction, that the path to holiness — which is to say the path to union with God — *passes by way of sexual healing and integration*, not around it. Because of the fallen world in which we live, we are all wounded in our sexuality; we are all cut off from its deepest truth and its mystical meaning. There is no getting around the painful process of sexual healing if we desire to enter the "great mystery" of "nuptial union" with God. This is true for everyone, regardless of one's state in life. Married, consecrated celibates, and single people alike are *all* called to sexual integration — to the healing of the rupture within us between body and soul, spirituality and sexuality.

Here we must be clear that sex — maleness and femaleness and the call to union — is *not* God's wine cellar. Sexual union is *not* the union that ultimately satisfies our longing. Understanding the "great mystery" of human sexuality is *only the key* that opens us to the infinitely greater mystery of what John of the Cross called "mystical marriage" with God. The world is idolatrously fixated on the key, mesmerized by it. But — and this is the tragedy — *it doesn't know how to use it.* There we stand with key in hand at the locked gate, longing to enter the wild garden of delights (union with God), but we know not what the key is for. The key is stamped right in our sexual bodies, but we have not understood the mystic wisdom to which our bodies point. We are almost deaf to the Song our bodies invite us to sing.

The mystics are those who see the divine wisdom inscribed in all of creation, especially in the human body as male and female. They are the ones who have understood "the key" and have used it to gain access to the wine cellar of divine intoxication, to the enclosed garden of fertile delights. Mystics are the ones who hear the Song of Songs echoing in their hearts and have dared to allow themselves to enter into it, and to sing back to God, dancing wildly as David did before the ark (see 2 Sam 6).

But, as the saying goes, those who hear not the music think the dancers mad. Sadly, because of their boldness, because of the intense and sometimes "scandalous" nature of their lives, mystics have often been dismissed as out-of-touch, even dangerous. Teresa of Avila's commentary on the Song of Songs was considered so "scandalous" that a tragically misguided priest ordered her to burn it. "Throw this into the fire!" wrote Father Diego de Yanguas. "It is not decent for a woman to write about the Song" (cited in CL, p. 42). Certain Carmelites considered John of the Cross such a threat that they threw him into prison. And Louis de Montfort ruffled so many feathers that he suffered an attempt on his life by poisoning.

It is one thing to prefer a different type of spirituality from that proposed by a certain saint or mystic. But it is another to dismiss the mystical tradition as irrelevant. "Against those who dismiss [mystics like] St. John of the Cross as preoccupied with extraordinary and miraculous mystical phenomena that are irrelevant for ordinary believers," at the core of John Paul II vision is the belief "that St. John of the Cross's teachings concern the normal development of the supernatural life of faith and love" (Waldstein, TOB, p. 87). This doesn't mean we should all expect daily ecstasies or bodily levitations. But there is an "everyday mysticism" to which we are all called, an everyday encounter with the "great mystery" that is Christ and his love affair with us, his Bride, the Church – in good times and bad, sickness and health, dry spells and fervor, all the days of our lives. As the *Catechism* teaches, "God calls us all to this intimate union with him, even if the special graces or extraordinary signs of this mystical life are granted only to some for the sake of manifesting the gratuitous gift given to all" (CCC 2014). In other words, appealing to the imagery of the Song, God calls us *all* to enter his wine cellar in order to have our fill of his wine. *Every*one is invited mystically to enter the gates of the "garden closed." Everyone is called to enter into "heaven's song."

The Difficulty of Entering the Mystery

Speaking of this call to enter mystically into "the garden" (here again he sees Mary as the woman in the Song), St. Louis de Montfort remarks, "But how difficult it is for us sinners to have the freedom, the ability and the light to enter such an exalted and holy place" (TD 263). "Some," he says, "the great majority – will stop short at the threshold and go no further. Others – not many – will take but one step into its interior. Who will take a second step? Who will take a third? Finally who will remain in it permanently? Only the one to whom the Spirit of Jesus reveals the secret" (TD 119).

The "secret" of which de Montfort speaks is whispered throughout the Scriptures to all those with "ears to hear." We see it, among *many* other places, in David's deep longing to enter the courts of the Lord (see Ps 84); in Isaiah's joyous prophecy that the redeemed will "enter Zion with singing" (Is 35:10; 51:11); in Nicodemus' question about entering the womb a second time to be born anew (see Jn 3:3-8); in the healing of the lame man who enters "the Beautiful Gate" of the Temple leaping and praising God (Acts 3:1-10); and in the heavenly promise that those who wash their robes will enter the City of God by the gates (Rev 22:14). "This is the gate of the Lord; the righteous shall enter through it!" (Ps 118:20). But this "secret" of which de Montfort speaks is whispered especially in the Song of Songs. Elsewhere, this French mystic writes,

> Fortunate and happy, incredibly happy, is the soul to which the Holy Spirit reveals the Secret.... To that soul the Paraclete opens the "Garden Enclosed." He permits it to drink deep draughts of the living waters of grace from the "Fountain Sealed"! That soul will find God alone in his most glorious garden. It will find God infinitely holy and exalted yet adapting Himself to the weakness of the soul. (SM, p. 17)

Oh, what glorious divine condescension! God comes right down to our level in the "garden" of Mary's womb. This, according to de Montfort, is where we meet God and he meets us.

If we are to meet Christ in the Mystery of his Incarnation, nay more, if we are to be *formed into "other Christs"* we must pour ourselves, mystically speaking, like molten liquid into Mary's womb; we must have the courage to enter mystically behind the veil into her "enclosed garden" – the perfect mold that formed the God-Man. As de Montfort puts it:

> A sculptor has two ways of making a statue. He may carve it ... [or] he may cast it in a mold. An unhappy blow of the hammer or a slip of the chisel ... may destroy the carver's work .... Casting in a mold requires little work, little time, little expense. And if the mold be perfect ... it forms the desired figure quickly, easily, and gently – provided the material used does not resist the operation. Mary, the great and unique mold of God, was made by the Holy Spirit to form the God-man, the man-God. In this mold, none of the features of the Godhead is missing. Therefore, whosoever is cast into it, and yields himself to the molding, receives all the features of Jesus Christ. (SM, pp. 15-16)

I think it is safe to say that John Paul II conceived of his TOB precisely from "within" Mary's womb, in the mystical sense described above. For her womb is "the house of the divine secrets" (TD 264), and the TOB provides the key to this house, unfolding for us these "divine secrets." We must remember that "the de Montfort way" profoundly influenced John Paul II's particular spirituality. His papal motto, *Totus Tuus* (totally yours), referred precisely to this idea of pouring himself out totally *for* Mary and *in* Mary so as to be formed into another Christ – or, in his case, to be formed into a true Vicar of Christ. The holiness of John Paul II radiated precisely as a result of his deep intimacy with this woman, his deep familiarity with the "untold riches, beauties, rarities, and delights" of Mary's garden (TD 261). At Mary's "virginal bosom" John Paul II was "nourished with the milk of her grace" (TD 264). It is there, "in the bosom of Mary," that we "grow mature in enlightenment, in holiness, in experience and in wisdom" (TD 156). "It is upon [Mary's] breast," in fact, as de Montfort says, "that all good things come to me" (TD 216).

Here, we can marvel at the deep comfort St. Louis de Montfort exhibits towards the body. With great reverence and a kind of "holy daring," he unabashedly presents the spiritual mystery revealed to us through the Virgin Mary's feminine body. If we don't share his comfort – indeed, many find themselves decidedly *uncomfortable* in the face of such a treatment of Mary – we would do well to examine the source of such discomfort. It is much easier to eschew the body (our own body, Jesus' body, Mary's body) than it is to face the disorders in our hearts that cause us to eschew the body. But we needn't fear those disorders. Rather, with a humble willingness to receive her good counsel, we can and should surrender our disorders to Mary, to the purifying furnace of love that is her womb. All the base metals thrown into this "blazing furnace of love," according to de Montfort, melt down and change into gold (see TD 261).

Personal impressions of Mary as somehow "above" the earthiness of her own body (as if devotion to her demanded that we eschew her body or our body or both) can only stem from projecting our own dis-integrated "body issues" on to her. *Mary has no "body issues"!* She is a *fully* redeemed woman, the New Eve. That means *she has none of our hang-ups with the body and its sexuality.* She doesn't respond to the world's sexual impropriety by going to the other extreme (prudery), as we are often inclined to do. She knows all the secrets of heaven's song, and she longs to share them with us in order to free us from the lies we have believed and enable as to live our sexuality as it was meant to be.

If we find ourselves uncomfortable pondering the beauty and mystery of Mary's body, perhaps it stems from memories of our own mothers and their attitudes about the body. For those of us with "mother wounds," Mary's fully integrated motherhood is a glorious, healing balm. *Mary loves her body!* She rejoices eternally in "the womb that bore [Christ] and the breasts [he] sucked" (Lk 11:27). And she longs to share her loving-nurturing-spiritual-body-goodness with all of her children. She rejoices to carry us mystically in her womb, nurse us mystically at her breasts, fondle us, cuddle us, sing to us. And whenever we stink up our lives with sin, she doesn't scold, she doesn't shame – she happily and readily changes our diapers, wiping our bottoms clean with her tender love and mercy (which is God's tender love and mercy). For Mary also loves *our* bodies and yearns to teach us how to love them. As Father Donald Calloway puts it:

> Mary shows us how to accept the gift of our embodiedness,
> and this includes the God-given sex of the body. In this
> it is important to note that Mary's exemplarity of what
> it means to accept the gift of one's body means that the
> body is not an obstacle to overcome but, rather, a gift to

be lived. Mary delights in her body, especially in its God-given sex: femininity. It is precisely in her gift of being a woman that Mary was fashioned and called by God to be the *Theotokos* [God-bearer]. The gift of her body is exactly what helps her to become the *Theotokos*. Just think of what would have happened if Mary had rebelled against the gift of her feminine body! *We* would be in a very different situation today. (MTB, pp. 55-56)

Mary's feminine body points us to a great spiritual mystery. If Mary is to be our Mother in the order of grace, then we must allow ourselves to be "born again" from her "blessed womb" and we must draw sustenance, as Christ did, from her "blessed breasts" (see Lk 11:27). This is how we become the "children of God" we are meant to be. Being mothered by Mary in this way is obviously not a physical reality for us, as it was for Christ. We are Mary's spiritual children. As such, St. Peter tells us we should "long for pure spiritual milk" (1 Pet 2:2). Still, it is entirely fitting to look to the bodily reality of Mary's motherhood – as de Montfort leads us to do – to reveal to us the spiritual mystery. This, of course, is precisely what the TOB teaches us: "The body, in fact, and only the body, is capable of making visible what is invisible: the spiritual and the divine" (TOB 19:4). In order to see the spiritual mystery revealed through Mary's body, however, our diseased notions about the body (in this case, the female body) must be exposed, confessed, and healed. We must be purified, our hearts radically transformed. As John Paul II unfolds in great detail throughout his TOB, this transformation occurs as we enter more and more fully into the "great mystery" of "the redemption of our bodies" (Rom 8:23).

This is a mystical journey – a journey that is, as the Pope tells us, "totally sustained by grace." At the same time, it "demands an intense spiritual commitment [on our part] and is no stranger to painful purifications (the 'dark night'). But it leads, in various possible ways," as we already quoted John Paul saying, "to the ineffable joy experienced by the mystics as 'nuptial union.' How can we forget here, among the many shining examples, the teachings of St. John of the Cross and St. Teresa of Avila?" (NMI 33).

My Beloved Is Mine and I Am His

The defining element of "mystical marriage," according to John of the Cross, is the total surrendering of God to the soul and the soul to God, such that the two "belong" to each other in the manner of spouses. The Mystical Doctor writes that in this surrender a "reciprocal love is thus actually formed between God and the soul, like the marriage union and surrender, in which the goods of both ... are possessed by both together. They say to each other what the Son of God spoke to the Father ... All that is mine is yours and yours is mine [Jn 17:10]" (CW, p. 706).

We see this mutual "belonging" to each other very clearly in the Song of Songs: "My beloved is mine and I am his" (2:16). In the language of authentic love, when spouses speak of "belonging" to each other, it does not and cannot refer to an impersonal "ownership" of one by the other. Rather, it "indicates the reciprocity of giving, it expresses the equilibrium of the gift ... in which the reciprocal *communion of persons* is established" (TOB 33:4). As John Paul states: "When the bride says, 'My beloved is mine,' she means at the same time, 'It is he to whom I entrust myself,' and therefore she says, 'and

I am his' (Song 2:16)" (TOB 110:9). The words "my" and "mine," according to the Holy Father, affirm the whole *depth of the entrustment* in a way that corresponds to the inner truth of the person who, as a person, must never be dominated or "owned" (see TOB 110:9).

Interestingly, this reciprocal "belonging" and "entrustment" seems to be generated above all from masculine desire, the Pope observes. For the bride repeats continually, "his desire is for me" (7:10). But the bride has a reciprocal desire and, recognizing his purity, a trusting acceptance of his desire (see TOB 113:1). Correspondingly, in the relationship between God and man, it is God who first desires man: "This is love, not that we loved God, but that he first loved us" (1 Jn 4:10). The original and natural disposition of humanity as "bride" is that of open, trusting acceptance of God's initiation of love. Tragically, however, at the prompting of the Deceiver, the bride in Genesis came to see God as a tyrant with a will to rule over her, dominate her – violate her. In light of this deception, we must ask: Why would God create his bride as "inviolable" only to violate her?

If the lover of the Song is an image of the Divine Bridegroom, then God, too, respects his bride as "master of her own mystery." Wojtyla makes this point unambiguously clear in the following provocative statement:

> Nobody can use a person as a means toward an end, no human being, nor yet God the Creator. On the part of God, indeed, it is totally out of the question, since, by giving man an intelligent and free nature, he has thereby ordained that each man alone will decide for

himself the ends of his activity, and not be a blind tool of someone else's ends. Therefore, if God intends to direct man toward certain goals, he allows him to begin with to know those goals, so that he may make them his own and strive toward them independently. In this amongst other things resides the most profound logic of revelation: God allows man to learn his supernatural ends, but the decision to strive toward an end, the choice of course, is left to man's free will. God does not redeem man against his will. (LR, p. 27).

And so the spousal imagery of the Song works on various levels. If we, in one sense, are to enter the mystery of the "garden enclosed" (the mystical womb of Mary, where we are formed into "other Christs"), we, too, in another sense, should be ready to open the garden of our hearts immediately when the Bridegroom comes home from the marriage feast and knocks (see Lk 12:36). "Behold, I stand at the door and knock; if any one hears my voice and opens the door, I will come in to him and eat with him, and he with me ... He who has an ear, let him hear" (Rev 3:20, 22).

If Christ is the true Bridegroom of the Song, then it is he who knocks at the garden gate of our souls, crying out to us as he does, "Open to me, my sister, my love, my dove, my perfect one, for my head is wet with dew" (5:2). This is "divine dew falling from heaven to make the soul fruitful," according to de Montfort (TD 253), so that God's Son may be conceived in us, as he was in Mary. Let it be done, Lord, according to your word! Amen.

Mary, you opened yourself with abandon to the dew that fell from heaven, making your womb infinitely fruitful. Teach us, we beg you, not to fear to open ourselves to that same divine life. May we not fear the fire that Christ came to cast upon the earth. Rather, may we throw ourselves into it with confident abandon, as you did, Mary. Amen.

Kathy's upbringing had given her the impression that Mary's holiness and virginity somehow made her "unreachable" and "unapproachable" – especially when it came to sexual matters. As we corresponded more about all this via email, Kathy wrote: "I can only imagine the 'all pure' Mary turning her nose up at me, filled with utter disgust." I insisted that this could *not possibly be Mary's reaction.* Mary is the Mother of Mercy. She does what Christ does, and Christ was filled with a particular compassion and mercy for women caught in sexual sin.

I got the impression from several of Kathy's comments that she, like many, thought Mary's immaculate purity made her a prudish or even an "a-sexual" being without any hint of erotic feelings or desires. She said, "Well, what else am I supposed to think. That's certainly the impression I got from the nuns who taught me growing up." The following is an excerpt from my response:

Kathy, I was actually given a similar impression as a child. Of course, I think we need to be careful not to make generalizations or fall into "nun-bashing." God bless the countless heroic religious women who have witnessed faithfully through the ages to an authentic Catholic vision of life and love. But, truth be told, like you, I got a lot of wrong impressions about the faith growing up in Catholic schools. Only much later in life did I begin to understand that purity doesn't annihilate erotic desire, it perfects it.

Far from being "a-sexual," Mary is the only woman who ever experienced the fullness of God's original plan for sexuality. God made us male and female and called the two to become "one flesh" in order to point us to our ultimate destiny of union with God in Christ. *This* is the original and fundamental meaning of human sexuality and this is how Mary must have experienced her womanhood, her sexuality – as a burning desire for union with God.

Through the gift of redemption, we can begin to reclaim this original truth, but even for the holiest among us it remains muddled to some degree by our fallen condition. To recognize Mary as the "Immaculate One" is to recognize that her sexuality was never muddled by our fallen condition. For she experienced the *fullness of redemption* right from the first moment of her conception. This would mean that Mary's purity allowed her to experience her sexuality in its fullness – as a deep yearning for total communion with God in Christ. This is why she didn't have sexual relations with Joseph: not because marital union is "unholy," but because she was already living the union *beyond* sexual union – union with God. This is not to knock Joseph, but earthly, sexual union with him would have been for Mary *a step backwards*. Instead, Mary took Joseph *forward with her* into the fulfillment of all desire.

A few more emails followed, but Kathy remained skeptical of what I was trying to explain to her. Several months later, I received the following email, which Kathy (again, not her real name) has given me permission to reprint here in its entirety. I will let you judge for yourself what you think it means.

You may not remember me. I was the woman who thought Mary was disgusted by me when I got caught cheating on my husband. I've been reading the book you recommended and listening to some CD's. And I've been thinking a lot about what you told me about the Blessed Mother. The other night I had a dream. I was the woman caught in adultery in that Bible story. The people who wanted to throw stones at me where different people from my life – my parents, my grandmother, my husband, and a bunch of nuns from the order that taught at my grade school. They had the exact pre-Vatican II habit they wore when I was in the third grade. There were also some freaky skeleton-like creatures scurrying around on the ground (you know how weird dreams can be). Jesus said that anyone without sin could cast the first stone. Everyone left and dropped their stones except one of the nuns. I looked at Jesus and he said, "She's without sin. She can throw a stone if she wants." She was mean and old and had nasty whiskers growing out of her chin. I looked back at Jesus, and he just smiled. When I looked back again at the nun, she was radiant, glowing, young and alive, and a great beam of light was shining from between her breasts, coming from a ball of fire in her heart. I knew it was Mary. She gestured to me to look between my breasts. I looked down and saw a great ball of fire there too. Then I looked at Jesus and his heart was also a glowing ball of fire. Then she disappeared and I was alone with Jesus. The fire of his heart drew me to him, making the fire in my heart blaze all the more, and we embraced.

Reflection Questions

I. In this chapter we observed that there is no detour around the painful process of sexual healing and integration if we desire to enter into the great mystery of "nuptial union" with God. Where am I in need of sexual healing and integration? What memories might I need to open up to God's light for healing? Do I believe Christ *can* heal me and *wants* to?

2. What is my impression of the Blessed Mother? Do I consider her "above the body"? Do I consider her "a-sexual"? Is it difficult to imagine Mary rejoicing in her feminine body? If so, why? Where do these anti-body ideas come from?

3. Spend some time alone in a quiet place and ask Mary to speak to your heart about who she is and how she feels about her body and your body. Perhaps you might want to use the prayer below to help.

Suggested Prayer

Mary, Mother of God and my Mother, you were filled with *holy desire* for God and you are filled with *holy desire* for me — that I would come to know who I truly am as a son/daughter of God and as your son/daughter. Speak to my heart in a way that I can hear. Tell me how you feel about your body, about being a woman, about having borne the Christ-child and having nourished and nurtured him at your breasts. Tell me how you feel about my body and show me the path to deep integration of my body and soul. Amen.

Chapter 5

The Language of the Body is "Gift"

Josh was excited about his budding relationship with Jessica — but for all the wrong reasons. After a string of boyfriends, Jessica had gained quite a "reputation" on campus. Guys were clamoring for her attention, and Josh had it.

Josh was imagining he would date her for a couple months, have his "fun," and then break up. This, anyway, seemed to be the pattern in Jessica's life, and Josh was fine with that. He wasn't looking for any kind of committed relationship.

After a weekend of "messing around" with Jessica, Josh made the casual comment: "I hope when this is all over, we can still be friends." Only one word came out of Jessica's mouth: "*Over?!*" But her eyes made the rest of her sentiments very clear: *You mean you're just another one of those jerks who's in it for his own kicks, and in a few weeks I'm going to be abandoned ... again?*

Josh knew that Jessica had pegged him. He wasn't in it for the long haul. He was just looking for some "fun." But what was he to say, "Yes, you're right. I'm just a user"? So, in order to save face, he put it back on her: "I was just kinda thinkin' that that was what *you* might want ... you know, nothing long-term ... 'cause that's how your other relationships have been." Jessica responded with a desperate tell-me-it-isn't-so kind of look: "But *this* isn't like my other relationships, Josh. We're

different. This is *real* love and *real* love lasts forever." – "Forever
... forever ... forever ..." Josh can still hear that fateful word
ringing in his ears.

What began as an attempt to save face turned into a
six-year dating relationship, the last five of which they lived
together. Josh managed to get what he wanted out of the
arrangement, and Jessica had the sense of permanence. But
the "sense" wasn't enough. She wanted a ring. Josh, somewhat
reluctantly, resigned himself to that fate.

> *"I shall remain totally engrossed in your Secret ..."*
> – From "The Mother" by Karol Wojtyla

In the previous chapter, we dared to ponder the "opening" of the
great mystery of that "enclosed garden." Now we must be even
more daring as we continue our journey – daring *and* reverent. What
lies within is *so glorious... so stupendous... so holy...* that if we presume to
reach out and "touch" this mystery without the proper reverence,
we can expect the fate of Uzzah who was "struck down" when
he reached out to touch the ark of the Old Covenant without the
proper respect (see 2 Sam 6). How much more reverence is required
if we are to "touch" – even more, to enter mystically into – the ark
of the New Covenant, the mystery of "the woman" of the Song of
Songs, the mystery of Mary? Does this perhaps explain why Joseph
was afraid to take Mary into his home (see Mt 1:20)?

What, then, gives us entrance into so holy a mystery? We "have
confidence to enter the sanctuary by the blood of Jesus, by the new and

living way which he opened for us through the curtain, that is, through his flesh." So "let us draw near with a true heart in full assurance of faith, with our hearts sprinkled clean ... and our bodies washed with pure water" (Heb 10:19-22). And let us, with John Paul II, become "totally engrossed" in Mary's Secret!

What can we expect if we, with "a true heart," dare to enter this sanctuary, this Holy of all Holies, through the curtain opened for us by Christ (see Mk 15:38)? St. Louis de Montfort tells us that within this "enclosed garden," within this divine dwelling place, "there are trees planted by the hand of God ... beautiful flowers ... meadows verdant with hope, impregnable towers of fortitude, enchanting mansions of confidence, and many other delights" (TD 261). These are the delights for which we are created and for which we all yearn. We know something already of what lies within, for there is an imprint of the mystery within the human heart, and that imprint beckons – "Come! Come to the source and satisfaction of your yearning!" We intuit that, unless the God who made us is ruthless and cruel, the unyielding thirst of the human heart must lead eventually to an unending fountain of delight and satisfaction. We *must*, in fact, believe in such a gift, lest we commit the original sin all over again.

Grasping vs. Receiving the Gift

The authentic love sung in the Song of Songs is nothing other than a proper recognition, a proper "rereading," as John Paul says, of the true "language" that God inscribed in our bodies as male and female. That language is "gift" and "self-gift" (see TOB 111:4). "This is *the body*," John Paul asserts, "*a witness* to creation as a fundamental gift, and therefore a witness *to Love as the source from which this same giving springs"* (TOB 14:4). God's Love is the motivation of the very gift of our existence, and we exist *as male and female* precisely so we can image that same love by being a gift to one another. And so the Pope states that masculinity and femininity – namely, sex – is the original sign in the world of God's self-giving love. "This is the meaning with which sex enters into the Theology of the Body" (TOB 14:4).

As we observed earlier, a man's body makes no sense by itself. A woman's body makes no sense by itself. Seen in light of each other, we discover the unmistakable plan of the Creator: man and woman are destined to be a life-giving "gift" to one another, a gift that serves as a "created version" of the Uncreated Mystery of self-giving love between the Father, the Son, and the Holy Spirit. But, as we have already seen, if men and women are to live in the mystery of "gift," they cannot extort the gift, they cannot take or grasp at what is not freely given. Such grasping, in fact, is what constitutes the very nature of sin.

"So when the woman saw that the tree was good for food, and that it was a delight to the eyes, and that the tree was to be desired to make one wise, she took of its fruit and ate" (Gen 3:6). Interestingly, the woman of the Song also speaks of a tree that was "good for food," of taking delight in it, and of eating its sweet fruit: "As an apple tree among the trees of the wood, so is my beloved among young men. With great delight I sat in his shadow and his fruit was sweet to my taste" (2:3). Eve sins and the woman of the Song doesn't. What's the difference? It is that of *grasping* at the fruit versus *receiving* it as a gift.

Here we diverge a bit from John Paul's reflections on the Song so as to return to them with deeper insight and clarity. When God said they were not to eat from the "tree of the knowledge of good and evil," it cannot be said that God did not want to *give* them that fruit. God certainly wants us to have a knowledge of what is good and what is evil. But this knowledge (this fruit) is something at which we cannot grasp. We cannot invent good and evil for ourselves. We can only *receive* the knowledge of good and evil as something *given* to us by God. It seems the precise sin, then, was not the eating of the fruit of this particular tree. As we have just observed, God certainly wants to *give* us such knowledge ("fruit") as a gift. Rather, the sin seems to be the doubting of God's benevolence, the doubting and denial of his love, the doubting of his gift. We *want* the knowledge of good and evil ("the tree was good for food ... a delight to the eyes ... to be desired to make one wise," Gen 3:6), but we don't believe God will *give* us such knowledge, so we *grasp*. John Paul, in fact, describes the original sin as man's "casting doubt in his heart on the deepest meaning of the gift" (TOB 26:4).

Eve, having accepted the *paradigm of denial*, cast doubt on the gift of the Heavenly Bridegroom (Yahweh) and grasped at the fruit. The bride in the Song lives in the *paradigm of gift* and opens herself to receive the "fruit" which her bridegroom freely bestows upon her. If the bride in the Song is a type of Mary, then this New Eve has redeemed the first Eve's sin — not by refusing to eat the fruit, but by refusing to *grasp* at it. Eve doubted the gift, yet still yearning for it, she reached out to take it for herself; the New Eve believed in the gift, and "waited on the Lord" in her yearning. What Eve took to herself, the New Eve received as a gift from God.

And just as Eve offered the stolen fruit to Adam, Mary offers the divinely given fruit to us, encouraging us to "repent and believe" in the gift. In other words, it seems that what both the first Eve and the New Eve offer humanity is fruit of the same tree, just differently acquired. The first acquired through denial and grasping, the second acquired through faith and receptivity. Eve's fruit rots and leads to death, though, because it is cut off from its source. Mary's fruit flourishes, indeed multiplies into an abundant harvest, because it remains forever united with its source.

The Garden of Eden, as St. Louis de Montfort points out, was a type of Mary. Adam's birth from the virgin soil of Eden foreshadowed the New Adam's birth from the virgin soil of Mary. Looking at the Sumerian and Greek words for Eden/paradise takes us even deeper into the mystery. The Sumerian word *eden* means "fertile plain" or "fertile land." In Greek, *parádeisos* means a "pleasure park," a place of great delight. Eden, then, can be understood as the "garden of fertile delights." And Mary, as de Montfort draws out of such imagery, "is herself the earthly paradise, that virgin and blessed land from which sinful Adam and Eve were expelled" (TD 45). Furthermore, this garden of fertile delight "is guarded not by a cherub, like the first earthly paradise, but by the Holy Spirit himself ... Referring to her [the Holy Spirit] says, 'You are an enclosed garden and a sealed fountain.' Mary is enclosed. Mary is sealed. The unfortunate children of Adam and Eve, driven from the earthly paradise, can enter this new paradise only by a special grace of the Holy Spirit" (TD 263).

Mary alone, as "master of her own mystery" (TOB 110:7) "gives to the unfortunate children of unfaithful Eve entry into that earthly paradise where they may walk pleasantly with God," de Montfort states. "There they can feed without fear of death on the delicious fruit of the tree of life and," as the mystic adds plainly, "on the delicious fruit of ... *the tree of the knowledge of good and evil*" (TD 45, emphasis added). What? We can eat from the tree of the knowledge of good and evil without fear of death? Yes! How? By *believing* in the gift and *waiting* on the Lord to offer it to us according to his purpose and plan.

Eve was not mistaken when she saw that the fruit of the tree "was good for food" and "a delight to the eyes" (Gen 3:6). Why, then, were they not to eat of it? The Lord was not asking the first man and woman to deny any genuine yearning of their hearts. Rather, he was inviting them to enter into *deep trust* in his benevolence, deep trust in his *gift*. He was inviting the bride (all of mankind) to believe in and open to his spousal gift of self. Those who do so will "taste and see that the Lord is good!" (Ps 34:8). This is the mystery of "gift" and "trust" lived by the lovers in the Song of Songs.

Taste and See the Goodness of the Lord

John Paul quotes the entirety of the following passage from the Song (see TOB 111:4). If we follow the sensual imagery where it intends to lead us, we will come to "taste" and "see" the Lord's goodness.

> I said I will climb the palm tree
> and lay hold of its clusters of dates.
> Oh, may your breasts be for me like clusters of grapes,
> and the scent of your breath like apples.
> Your palate is like exquisite wine
> that flows directly to my beloved,
> and glides over lips and teeth. (Song 7:8–9)

And immediately the bride responds:

> I am my beloved's [or for my beloved],
> and his desire is for me.
> Come, my beloved,

let us go into the fields,

and pass the night in the villages.

Let us go out early in the morning to the vineyards;

we will see whether the vines have budded,

whether the flowers have opened

and the pomegranates are in bloom:

there I will give you my caresses. (Song 7:10–13)

In this erotic dialogue, the lovers discover each other as an exquisite gift and, as John Paul observes, they even "taste" each other as a gift — that is, the gift of the other is received through the bodily senses. Here we see how clearly the "*'language of the body' speaks to the senses.*" In other words, as John Paul observes, "The love that unites them is of a spiritual and sensual nature together" (TOB 111:5). This means their spiritual love is integrated with and even rooted in their bodies — in their sexuality and sensuality. The pining of their hearts for authentic love is expressed in the pining of their bodily senses, apparently without the disturbance and "disconnect" of lust. In this way, because of the very nature of sacramental reality, their *spiritual senses* are in a way accessed and awakened by their *physical senses*. In other words, they "taste and see the goodness of the Lord" precisely by tasting and seeing the goodness *of each other* in the intimate and sensual mystery of their union.

The erotic poetry of the Song of Songs is full of sensual references to foods and fragrances, to smelling, tasting, eating, and drinking each other's goodness (see, for example, 1:12–14; 2:3–6; 4:10–5:1). This indicates a profound interconnection between spousal love, smelling, tasting, eating, and drinking. Are not these senses (and, in fact, all of the senses) fully engaged in erotic love? What does the passionate kiss of lovers say if not in some sense "I want to taste you; I want to take you into myself and consume you; 'eat' you; 'drink' you"? Furthermore, does not the very fragrance of the body stir men and women to love? The lovers of the Song are intoxicated, spellbound by each other's aroma. "While the king was on his couch, my nard [perfume] gave forth its fragrance" (1:12). "His cheeks are like beds of spices, yielding fragrance" (5:13).

Perhaps we look on the senses with suspicion because they often rouse lust. In fact — because of the fallen, disintegrated state of our humanity — our senses almost inevitably incline us to lust. Does this mean we should ignore, squash, or otherwise obliterate our senses? No! It means we must seek integration. We must be willing to "pass-over" with Christ into the "life of the Spirit." This *does not* mean eschewing our bodies or ignoring our senses. But it does mean a willingness to "die" to our disordered desires. This "death" is not for death's sake; rather, we die to lustful sensuality so that *holy desire* might be resurrected in us. We must open our bodies — our entire body-soul humanity — to the indwelling of the Spirit. We must allow our physical senses to be *permeated* and *penetrated* by the Holy Spirit. To the degree that men and women draw their love from the fire of the Holy Spirit, their senses stir them to love as God loves. Yes, our senses — all of our senses — were created by God to inspire love!

This is the very nature of incarnational/sacramental reality. In light of the mystery of the Incarnation, all depreciations of the body and sensuality crumble. Christ's bodily existence teaches us, as Pope Benedict XVI says, "that the senses belong to faith." Christ "does not abolish them, but leads them to their original purpose" (SL, p. 123). God gave us bodily senses precisely so we could sense his incarnate love. Thus, St. John speaks of God's mystery as that which we have "*heard* [with our ears] ... *seen* with our eyes ... and *touched* with our hands" (I Jn I:I). This hearing, seeing, and touching continues today through the Church's sacraments and liturgical life. We see the interconnections between spousal love, smelling, tasting, eating, and drinking very clearly in the spousal mystery of the Eucharist. "*The Eucharist*," John Paul tells us, "*is the ... sacrament of the Bridegroom and of the Bride.*" It serves in some way "to express the relationship between man and woman, between what is 'feminine' and what is 'masculine'" (MD 26). It seems the deepest desire of the Heavenly Bridegroom is that we, the members of the Church, his Bride, might *eat his flesh* and *drink his blood* ("I have earnestly desired to eat this passover with you," Lk 22:I5). In the Eucharist, Christ the Bridegroom quite literally invites his Bride to "taste and see" his own goodness. He invites her to take his body and blood within her and thereby conceive eternal life.

In the liturgy, the fragrances of incense, oils, and candles all add to the sensual experience of the union of Bridegroom and Bride. Yes, Catholicism is something we *sense* – it is something we *feel, taste, hear, see, inhale.* As the *Catechism* teaches, "The need to involve the senses in [our life of] prayer corresponds to a requirement of our human nature" (CCC 2702).

Our physical senses, of course, are meant to serve as a spring board to our spiritual senses. Think about it: if the body makes spiritual realities visible (see TOB I9:4), then it follows that each of the physical senses point to a spiritual sense. Hence, the mystics speak of the spiritual senses of seeing, hearing, tasting, touching and smelling God. The very physical and sensual poetry of the Song is meant to catapult us into deep spiritual intimacy with the mystery of Christ – it is meant to catapult us into the "mystical marriage" of God with humanity, Christ with his Church. To enter in truly, we must experience the integration of spirituality and sensuality. We must allow our senses to speak. But we must not stagnate there. Entering the mystical marriage is a matter of "proceeding from the visible to the invisible, from the sign to the thing signified, from the 'sacraments' to the 'mysteries'" (CCC 1075). How do we proceed in this direction? Again, we must "pass-over" from death to life by surrendering entirely to the mystery of Christ's death and resurrection.

Love is "Strong as Death"

A mature integration of the spiritual and sensual realities of spousal love is indispensable if men and women are to read – or, as John Paul II says, "reread" – the language of the body truthfully. An emphasis on the spiritual realm to the neglect of the sensual realm would dis-incarnate love, trapping it in a state of spiritual paralysis. "Love," in this case, would become cold, distant, aloof, prudish, and inhuman. Emphasis on the sensual realm to the neglect of the spiritual realm would lead to the mere indulgence of sensuality without respect for the dignity of the persons involved. "Love," in this case, would amount to mutual use for pleasure.

As we have seen, the lovers of the Song witness to the proper integration of the spiritual and the sensual in their love. In this way "the rereading of the spousal meaning of the body in the truth is achieved, because the man and the woman together must constitute the sign of the reciprocal gift of self, which *sets the seal on their whole life*" (TOB 111:5). Consummation of the marriage is the specific moment in which the marriage bond is sealed and thereby rendered absolutely indissoluble by anything but death. To reread the language of the body truthfully, men and women must recognize that sexual intercourse proclaims: "I am totally yours unto death. I belong to you and you to me until death do us part." This is the *spiritual* content of their *sensual* union.

The bride confirms that she knows this truth when she says, "Set me as a seal upon your heart ... for love is strong as death ... Its flashes are flashes of fire, a most vehement flame. Many waters cannot quench love, neither can floods drown it. If a man offered for love all the wealth of his house, it would be utterly scorned" (8:6-7). John Paul says that these words bring us to "the peak" of the Song's declaration of love. They seem to present the final chords of the Song, the "final chords in the 'language of the body'." When we read that "love is strong as death" we discover "the closure and crowning of everything in the Song of Songs that begins with the metaphor of the 'garden closed' and of the 'fountain sealed'" (TOB 111:6).

With the metaphor of the closed garden and sealed fountain, the lover had presented himself to his beloved not as one superficially attracted to her feminine "otherness." Rather, he presented himself as one who was captivated and fascinated by her entire mystery as a woman, as one ready to uphold the whole personal dignity of her sex, as one desirous of honoring her as a feminine person, as a sister and a bride — until death.

Here we see that a woman can only open her "closed garden" to her lover and remain inviolate if she is assured that he is ready and willing to commit his *entire life* to her, if she is assured that he has set her *as a seal upon his heart*, if she is assured that his love will be *strong as death*. The woman must know that the "fire" of the man's desire, that the "vehement flame" in his heart is one of sincere love, not lust. The beloved of the Song is confident in the sincerity of her lover's gift. And so, in "the moment in which the bride of the Song of Songs ... asks, *'set me as a seal upon your heart,'* the whole delicate structure of spousal love *closes,* so to speak, in its own inner interpersonal circle" (TOB 111:6). In other words, the bride responds with the gift of herself, and in *opening* her garden to her bridegroom, an "inner interpersonal circle of love" *closes* around the spouses. We might even say that this circle encloses them *within her garden,* as it were.

This closure seems to speak of the exclusivity and fidelity essential to spousal love. As John Paul says, "It is in this closure [this exclusive, life-long commitment] that the visible sign of the ... sacrament matures." This sign of their union is "born of the 'language of the body,' reread, so to speak, to the end in the truth of [their] spousal love" (TOB 111:6). It is precisely in this commitment to reread the language of the body "to the end" that we see the power of the sacrament of marriage *really and truly* to communicate the mystery of Christ's love for the Church. For Christ committed himself to his bride "to the end" (Jn 13:1).

Spouses, however, must first open *to receive* this divine love if they are to share it with one another. They must enter the "great mystery" of Christ's spousal union with the Church so as to image it themselves. John Paul asks: "Could we even imagine human love without [Christ] the bridegroom and the love with which he first loved to the end? Only if husbands and wives share in that love and in that 'great mystery' can they love 'to the end.' Unless they share in it, they do not know 'to the end' what love truly is and how radical are its demands" (LF 19). "Love is strong as death." This is how radical are its demands. And Christ's love "unto death" is the definitive word on the subject. In turn, husbands are to love their wives "as Christ loved the church" (Eph 5:25).

Is this even possible? "With men this is impossible," Jesus says very plainly, "but with God all things are possible" (Mt 19:26). Loving as Christ loves is *certainly not* something that spouses can "muster up." Loving in this way is possible, John Paul tells us, "only as a result of a gift of God who heals, restores, and transforms the human heart by his grace" (VS 23). This means that holiness is not first something that we *do*. It is first something that we must allow to *be done unto us*. Holiness is Christ's *gift* to his Bride: "Christ loved the church and gave himself up for her ... that she might be holy and without blemish" (Eph 5:25-27). This means that "holiness is measured according to the 'great mystery' in which the Bride responds with the gift of love to the gift of the Bridegroom" (MD 27). It is "Christ in us" who loves. Let us, then, like a bride, open wide the doors of our hearts to Christ!

I met Josh and Jessica at one of my seminars. Josh's parents, knowing their son's marriage was in trouble, had given them tickets to attend as a tenth anniversary present. Josh asked if he could have some time to talk with me, so I invited him to drive me to the airport after the seminar. Because of a delayed flight, we had a few hours together. As Josh unfolded his story, I thought of the Pope's reflections on the Song of Songs, particularly about "love as strong as death" and the woman's need for permanence if she is to "open her garden" and remain inviolate.

Jessica had been violated by many men who had used her sexually and then abandoned her. It seems she "hooked" Josh because she could not face the pain of being used and abandoned all over again. She desperately wanted Josh to "set her as a seal on his heart." She, rightly so, wanted to be loved *forever*. But Josh was bitter, understandably so, about being manipulated into the relationship and manipulated into marriage. Sixteen years later, Josh was ready, as he said, "to head for the hills. I've wanted to so many times. *I wanted to on the day she first said this would last forever!*"

Josh said he had taken a lot of notes at my seminar and had "never heard this before." There was even a bit of excitement in his voice. Josh was clear on how Jessica wounded him, which was an important piece of the puzzle – for women know how to use and manipulate men just as much as men know how to use and manipulate women. Still, I challenged him, in light of all he had learned that day, to examine how he, right from the start, had wounded Jessica. I tried to help him see that there are rich, rich treasures in a woman's heart that we, as men, need to open ourselves to and learn from. There was a *reason*, I insisted, that Jessica wanted their relationship to last forever. It's not that men don't feel the need for permanence – we do, I told him. But, in a way, this need gets awakened in a man's heart – or, if already awakened, strengthened – by "listening" and "entering into" the mystery of a woman's heart. She tends to feel the need for permanence more profoundly and – when permanence is lacking – more painfully.

Men often want women to conform to *their* (fallen) desire in the sexual sphere: pleasure without commitment. The only way women can possibly do this, however, is by rejecting an integral aspect of their own femininity: their fertility (contraception and abortion "enable" women to do this). But if men are to learn what it means to love, they must learn to conform their desires to the true language of the body in its declaration of "forever." Jessica was certainly wrong to manipulate Josh into this "forever." But Josh was wrong not to see that that was what *his body* was saying from the start. Conforming one's mind and heart to the true language of the body is a long and exacting work. Not everyone is ready or willing to embrace the task.

Reflection Questions

1. This chapter spoke of the mystery of original sin as a denial of God's gift. When we don't believe that God really wants to *grant* us the desires of our hearts, we "deny his gift" and *grasp* at what we desire for ourselves. In what ways might I have a disposition of "grasping" rather than "receiving"? How does this affect my relationship with God and with others?

2. Love is "strong as death." But we are not able to love in this way simply by "trying really hard." It is possible "only as a result of a gift of God who heals, restores, and transforms the human heart by his grace" (VS 23). Are there ways in which I'm trying to love on my own without opening my heart to God's healing grace?

3. Is love something I *grasp* at? Am I willing to make myself vulnerable before God in order to *receive* his love as a gift?

Do fears present themselves at the thought of being utterly dependent on God to satisfy the desires of my heart?

Suggested Prayer

Father, Son, and Holy Spirit, you live a life of eternal bliss in self-giving love. You created me to share in that love, to share in your own bliss. Forgive me for ever doubting your gift. Forgive me for all the ways I grasp at happiness, pleasure, comfort. Forgive me for all the ways I try to satisfy the hungers of my heart on my own rather than believing in your gift to me, rather than opening my desire to you and trusting in you to fulfill it. Jesus, I thirst. Bring me to the waters of life. Jesus, I hunger. Feed me with the bread of life. Jesus, I yearn for the ecstasy for which you created me. Intoxicate me with your sweet wine. Amen.

Chapter 6

Eros and Agape

Father Sam witnessed a lot of marriages at his busy suburban parish. Underneath his encouraging Irish smile, however, he entertained more than a bit of cynicism as the couple stood in his presence and professed their vows. His own parents had divorced when he was nine because of his father's infidelities.

"I lost it," says Father Sam, "when my dad told me that Cybil [his third wife] was leaving him for the same reason. All he could say when I called him on it was, 'I've never met a woman who could satisfy me.'"

John Paul concludes his reflections on the Song of Songs by examining the relationship of *eros* (human, erotic love) and *agape* (divine, sacrificial love). The Pope observes "that this biblical poem reproduces the human face of eros, its subjective dynamism as well as its limits and its end, with authenticity free from defects" (TOB 112:1). How desperately our world needs to reflect on an authentic eros free from defects! As we shall see, only agape can restore eros to its true grandeur; only agape can enable eros to overcome its limits. And if eros has a "human face," as John Paul says, agape has a divine one. In turn, these different "faces" of love meet in Christ, for he is "the human face of God and the divine face of man" (EA 67).

Based on this illuminating truth, we might also describe Christ as the *eros of God* and the *agape of man*. In the love of Christ the Bridegroom, these different faces of love become one "great mystery." As Pope Benedict XVI said, "God loves, and his love may certainly be called *eros*, yet it is also totally *agape*" (DC 9). An eros that is also totally agape – this is the goal of marital love and sexual union, and, hence, it is the journey of healing and purification that the sacrament of marriage calls us to and affords.

Longing for the True, Good, and Beautiful

In an earlier section of his catechesis, John Paul had examined eros in light of Christ's words about lust in the Sermon on the Mount. He asked whether eros merely refers to the lust which Christ condemns, or whether eros could also refer to that good and beautiful attraction of the sexes revealed "in the beginning" by original nakedness and the spousal meaning of the body (see TOB 47).

Ever determined to establish the fundamental goodness of human nature, including sexual desire and sensuality, John Paul refused to surrender the term eros to the distortion of lust. In this early section of his catechesis, the Pope creatively rehabilitated eros by appealing to Plato's philosophy. In Platonic usage, eros means the interior force that attracts us to the true, the good, and the beautiful. Within this perspective, eros opens toward an authentic and mature purity of heart. The Holy Father never tires of explaining in his TOB that Christ not only accuses the heart of lust, but also appeals to the heart to rediscover the goodness of God's original plan for sexuality. The gift of redemption, then, "means *the possibility and the necessity of transforming* what has been weighed down by the [lust] of the flesh" (TOB 47:5) so that we might experience sexual love as it was meant to be. As John Paul also wrote:

> It is necessary continually to rediscover the spousal meaning
> of the body and the true dignity of the gift in what is
> "erotic." This is the task of the human spirit.... If one does
> not assume this task, the very attraction of the senses and
> the passion of the body can stop at mere concupiscence
> [lust], deprived of all ethical value. [If man stops here, he]
> does not experience that fullness of "eros," which implies
> the upward impulse of the human spirit toward what is
> true, good, and beautiful, so that what is "erotic" also
> becomes true, good, and beautiful. (TOB 48:1)

You may recall the last sentence of this quotation from the
section of the Introduction in which we discussed the need to reclaim
the erotic realm for Christ. The more we do, the more we come to
experience the true grandeur of eros. And the more we experience the
true grandeur of eros, the more the cloud of negativity and shame that
tends to hover over all things sexual dissipates in our hearts. We no
longer tend to condemn manifestations of sexuality with a sense of
suspicion. Instead, the mystery of sexuality becomes a "sacramental"
revelation of the very meaning of life as a call to communion with
God and one another. And we know it is *very good*.

The Process of Tension and Search

For eros to be experienced as an aspiration toward what is true,
good, and beautiful, it must remain open to *agape*, as in a never ending
search for it. We witness this constant searching of eros for agape in
the verses of the Song of Songs. The erotic attraction of the lovers
expresses itself "in the frequent refrains that speak of the search full

of longing and of the spouses' reciprocal rediscovery. This brings them joy and calm, and at the same time seems to lead them to a new search, a continual search" (TOB 112:1).

John Paul observes that in their search for each other and even in their reaching each other, *"they ceaselessly continue to tend toward something"* (TOB 112:1). Their duet clearly shows their readiness to respond to the call of eros. But it also intimates that they desire *something more*. That "something more" is agape. In the end, God alone can satisfy the ache of human solitude: "It is not good that the man should be alone" (Gen 2:18). The best the communion of man and woman can be is a foretaste, a foreshadowing, a "sacrament" of the ultimate fulfillment that awaits us in the Marriage of the Lamb. Hence, in this life, love always involves a *"process of tension and search,"* as John Paul puts it (TOB 112:2). It is ever seeking and never satisfied. Every true lover can thus echo the lyrics of U2's famous song: "I still haven't found what I'm looking for...."

This process of tension and search is clearly expressed in the following verses of the Song: "Upon my bed by night I sought him whom my soul loves; I sought him, but found him not; I called him, but he gave no answer. I will rise now and go about the city ... I will seek him whom my soul loves" (3:1-2). Here we see that "human eros reveals the face of *love* ever *in search* and, as it were, *never satisfied*" (TOB 112:4). This kind of restlessness runs throughout the verses of the Song: "I opened to my beloved, but my beloved had turned and gone. My soul failed me ... I found him not; I called him but he gave no answer ... I am sick with love" (5:6, 8).

John Paul asks whether such restlessness is part of the nature of eros. Then he adds that if it is, "such restlessness would indicate ... *the need for [eros] to surpass itself*" (TOB 113:2), to go beyond its own limitations.

Authentic love extends to the furthest limits of the language of the body in order to overcome those limits (see TOB 113:3). The body, for all its wonders and glories, is, after all, a limited, finite reality. How can the finite human body possibly speak the language of an infinite love? How can eros overcome its bodily limitations so as to express agape?

Limitations in the Language of the Body

John Paul speaks of three limitations of eros: (1) *eros is limited by the body's weakness*, (2) *by the prospect of death*, and (3) *by jealousy*. Let's look at each of these limitations *and* at how spouses can overcome them.

(1) *Eros is limited by the body's weakness.*

When the bride in the Song exclaims, "I am sick with love," John Paul says it is as if she wanted to bear witness to her own fragility, to her own weakness. Earlier in his TOB, John Paul told us that man cannot fully express love without the body (see TOB 104:7). Now he states that due to the body's weakness, love — and here it seems he means the divine dimension of love (agape) — ultimately "shows itself *as greater than what the 'body' is able to express*" (TOB 112:5). For in the final analysis, the infinitude of Love is *too much* for the finitude of the body. A body that were to take it in would "break" — more aptly, "explode." Infinite Love inevitably *wounds* our finite humanity. And as we see in Christ, it is a mortal wound.

What *is* Christ the Bridegroom's passion and death if not the visible "explosion" of divine love *within* a human body? Might we look upon Christ's wounds — his bloody lacerations from the scourging, his flesh pierced by thorns, nails, and a sword — not only as *wounds of hatred* inflicted from "without," but also as *wounds of love* expressed from within? For within, "contained" in his beating heart, was something the human body *simply cannot contain* – the *infinite love* of the Trinity. Is it not *that love* that bursts through the pores of his brow in drops of blood, rends his flesh in multiple lacerations, punctures his hands and feet, and finally bursts the membranes of his heart in a gushing surge of blood and water? Is this not precisely the infinite love of the Trinity "exploding" in a human body?

And what of Mary? Her finite body also "contained" infinite love. He whom the universe cannot contain came to dwell in her body. And because of it, a sword of sorrow pierced her heart also (see Lk 2:35). Like Jesus and Mary, all who wish to experience and express divine love in their bodies, must "passover" into this divine mystery through suffering, making up in their own flesh what is "lacking" in the sufferings of Christ (see Col 1:24). For all those who accept this way as their own ("Take up your cross and follow..."), a sword of sorrow will pierce their hearts also. How can we not be reminded in this context of Bernini's famous statue "The Ecstasy of St. Teresa"? Memorialized in stone, we see the angel of love poised to thrust his wounding arrow into Teresa's readied heart. Her face – masterfully sculpted by Bernini – tells the story of a mystic who is tasting, as John Paul describes it, "the paradoxical blending of bliss and pain" as *"something akin to Jesus' experience on the Cross"* (NMI 27). And one would have to be either blind or ignorant not to notice that she looks like a bride in the climax of her nuptial union.

How, then, can spouses overcome the weakness of the body? Precisely by embracing the mortal wound of love, the body "passes over" to another dimension of love, experiencing something of the final reality when the mortal will be clothed with immortality (see 1 Cor 15:54). It is this "clothing" of the body with divine life that enables spouses to love as God loves, not only despite their bodies' weaknesses, but in some way, in and through those weaknesses. In other words, the very weakness of the body – its very *inability* to express the fullness of divine love – when humbly accepted, becomes itself in some way the body's *ability* to express that love. In this way the body's weakness itself proclaims the Christian paradox that "when I am weak, then I am strong" (2 Cor 12:10). In short, we needn't fear our human weaknesses – bodily or otherwise. By embracing them, by humbly accepting them and opening them to Christ, his strength works mightily in and through weakness.

We will look now at the second "limitation" of the language of the body.

(2) Eros is limited by the prospect of death.

"Love is strong as death" (Song 8:6). According to John Paul, these words express the power and force of erotic love to draw man and woman into a loving union – and it is precisely *from the depth of this union* that the words "Love is strong as death" come forth (see TOB 112:5). But these words also point, at least indirectly, to the fact that the love expressed in the "language of the body" finds its conclusive end in death (see TOB 112:5). Marriage itself is a commitment which ends with death. Can eros surpass death? Can the "language of the body" overcome the "strength" of the grave?

Early on in his catechesis, John Paul had said: "In man, consciousness of the meaning of the body ... come[s] into contact with the consciousness of death ... And yet, in man's history ... life struggles always anew with the inexorable prospect of death, and always overcomes it" (TOB 22:7). Now, in his reflections on the Song of Songs, John Paul observes that if the body conceals within itself the prospect of death, love does not want to submit to it. "In fact – as we read in the Song of Songs – love is 'a flame of the Lord' that 'the great waters cannot quench ... neither can the rivers drown it' (Song 8:6-7)." This poet-pope considers these words, among all the words of world literature, to be "particularly fitting and beautiful" (TOB 113:1). When eros opens itself to the "flame of the Lord" – that is, to agape – rivers cannot drown it; death cannot conquer it. "I have come to set the world ablaze," says Jesus (see Lk 12:49). When eros is inflamed with agape, "death is swallowed up in victory" (I Cor 15:54) and "love never ends" (I Cor 13:8). We will see this truth all the more clearly when we reflect on the marriage of Tobias and Sarah in the second part of this book.

But now, let's look at the third "limitation" of the language of the body.

(3) Eros is limited by jealousy.

In the same verse in which we discover that "love is strong as death," we also discover that love involves a "jealousy [that] is cruel as the grave" (8:6). Jealousy, from one perspective, confirms "*the exclusivity and indivisibility of love.*" That said, it "is nevertheless difficult to deny that jealousy manifests ... a spiritual kind of limitation" (TOB 113:1). It manifests a lack of trust, a lack of freedom, and a possessiveness not in keeping with the dignity of the person. It is true in a way that the spouses "belong" to each other ("My beloved is mine and I am his," 2:16). However, when this degenerates into a jealous "possession" of the other, authentic love "demands from both that they take a further step on the staircase of such belonging, always seeking a new and more mature form of it" (TOB 113:2).

The notion of climbing a staircase speaks to the ongoing and gradual ascent of love. "Love," as John Paul II put it, "should be seen as something which in a sense never 'is' but is always only 'becoming,' and what it becomes depends upon the contribution of both persons and the depth of their commitment" (LR, p. 139). If lovers tend toward jealousy, as they progresses in the ascent of love, in love's "becoming," jealousy gives way to a beautifully confident trust and freedom. Those who are utterly confident in the other's steadfast love are not jealous of his or her interactions with others. True love has cast out that fear of being replaced or "cheated on." They are living in authentic intimacy. But to reach this level of intimacy and trust, one cannot rely solely on the power of eros. When left to itself, erotic desire "is not able to pass beyond the threshold of jealousy" (TOB 113:1).

But here is the good news: erotic desire need not be left to itself. Eros can overcome the limit of jealousy by opening itself to agape. In light of the death and resurrection of Christ, St. Paul proclaimed that "Love is patient and kind; love is *not jealous*" (1 Cor 13:4). Where "human eros closes its own horizon" Paul's words open us to "another horizon of love that speaks another language." This love "seems to emerge from another dimension of the person," and invites us "to another [kind of] communion" (TOB 113:5) – the kind of communion that rests assured in fidelity and, hence, has been liberated from jealousy. "*This love has been called 'agape,'* and agape brings eros to fulfillment while purifying it" (TOB, p. 591).*

---

* This quotation is taken from the abridged catechesis delivered on June 6, 1984, which Waldstein also includes in his 2006 translation alongside the full text. Hence, the provision of a page number rather than an audience number.

Sign and Reality

By looking at the limitations of eros and the power of agape to enable men and women to overcome those limitations, we learn ever more deeply what it means to read the "language of the body" in truth. Although it is true that the erotic language of the body has limitations, it is *not true* that spouses are hopelessly bound by those limitations. Men and women can open their erotic desires to the eternal flame of agape and be liberated from the limitations of eros. We must, in fact, be liberated in this way if we are to constitute the sign of married love in truth. Indeed, if marriage is to be a true sacrament of divine love – which means an actual participation in and communication of divine love – then eros *must* express agape. Through this integration of eros and agape, spouses will be able *"to reach* what constitutes *the very nucleus of the gift of person to person"* (TOB 113:3). In other words, by continually opening eros to the ever-deepening penetration of agape, spouses reach ever-closer to the very core of spousal love – the reciprocal gift of one person to another in a bond that mirrors the very bond of the Trinity and that of Christ with the Church.

Still, the sacramental mystery of spousal union in the Song of Songs – as beautiful and wonderful as it is – remains only a sign, a mirror reflecting something of the divine Mystery. Even spouses must be open to "breaking away," the Pope says, from the earthly means of expressing eros-agape in order to reach that *nucleus of the gift of person to person* (see TOB 113:3). The ultimate reality of the gift of person to person can be none other than the relationship of Father and Son lived in the unity of the Holy Spirit. As the *Catechism* observes, "The personal relation of the Son to the Father is something that man cannot conceive of nor the angelic powers even dimly see: and yet, the Spirit of the Son grants a participation in that very relation to us who believe that Jesus is the Christ and that we are born of God" (CCC 2780).

Stunning. We are called to participate in the eternal "explosion" of love between the Father and the Son which is the Holy Spirit – a union of love that we cannot begin to fathom and the angels cannot even dimly see. And, yet, we do have some faint premonition of it. Pope Benedict XVI describes the eternal life that awaits us as "the supreme moment of satisfaction, in which totality embraces us and we embrace totality." It will be "like plunging into the ocean of infinite love ... a plunging ever anew into the vastness of being, in which we are simply overwhelmed with joy" (SS 12).

Only participation in *this* mystery of Love and Communion can satisfy the desire that is ever seeking and (in this life) never satisfied. What, then, is the purpose of the communion of man and woman, of eros, in this life? Building on all that John Paul II taught in his TOB, Pope Benedict says eros is meant to provide "a certain foretaste of the pinnacle of our existence, of that beatitude for which our whole being yearns." However, if eros is really to be a foretaste of the eternal union that awaits us, it "needs to be disciplined and purified" (DC 4). This is the role of agape – not to replace eros, but to restore it to its true grandeur (see DC 5).

In short, what we are realizing is that if eros is to become an earthly sign of that divine Communion, then the *language of the body* must be taken up into the *language of the liturgy*. It is precisely here, in the Church's liturgy – her life of prayer, of participation in the sacraments, and of worship – that the divine and human meet, that heaven and earth "kiss," that men and women come to participate in the divine nature (see 2 Pt 1:4).

But how can we possibly participate in God's own nature? Pope Benedict XVI asks: "Are not God and man completely incommensurable?

Can man, the finite and sinful one, cooperate with God, the Infinite and Holy One? Yes, he can, precisely because God himself has become man, become body, and here [in the liturgy], again and again, he comes through his body to us who live in the body" (SL, p. 173).

In the back of his mind, Father Sam wondered if he had chosen a life of celibacy out of fear: fear of the marriage commitment; fear that his father's proclivity for infidelity might be running through his own veins; fear of failure; and fear of putting children through the same hell that he had been through. "Becoming a priest," he said, "seemed like a good way to avoid all that."

Father Sam was ordained in 1979, the very year John Paul II started delivering his talks on the Theology of the Body. But it wasn't until 2006 that someone introduced him to John Paul II's teaching. "Where's this been all my years as a priest?" he wonders. The section on celibacy opened his eyes to a profoundly positive way of viewing his vocation – not as a hiding place from his fear, but as a way of living out an *eros* that was open to and integrated with *agape*. "I still have layers of stuff to work through here, but I can see God writing straight with my crooked lines," says Father Sam with a hopeful light in his eyes.

The section on the Song of Songs about the limits of eros as a love that is "ever seeking and never satisfied" also shed light on his father's life-long struggle. "For cryin' out loud! My dad is right, in a way. No woman *can* satisfy him. He's looking for an infinite love that no woman can possibly satisfy, that no woman was meant to satisfy. It has actually given me an open door to share the Gospel with my dad. There's a hard shell there, but I actually think he's listening to me."

Father Sam also says he has noticed that he is less cynical now as he prepares couples for marriage. "I tell them flat out that they're in for trouble if they think their marriage is going to satisfy their deepest yearning for love. Not gonna happen. Only if they set their sights on the marriage of heaven can they find the love they're looking for. Then they are able to live their marriage as a sacrament. Over the years I've seen husbands who are jealous because their wives love Jesus more than them. Only if spouses love God more than each other do they know how to love each other in the right way. John Paul's teaching has made this quite clear for me."

Reflection Questions

1. John Paul II says that eros "implies the upward impulse of the human spirit toward what is true, good, and beautiful, so that what is 'erotic' also becomes true, good, and beautiful" (TOB 48:1). What feelings or sentiments are triggered in my heart by connecting the word "erotic" with the words "true, good, and beautiful"?

2. Do I really believe that the erotic realm can become something "true, good, and beautiful," a privileged path for experiencing union with God?

3. Are there ways in my life in which I have "idolized" the body and sex? In other words, have I looked to the sexual realm to satisfy a hunger in my heart that only God can satisfy?

Suggested Prayer

Jesus, you came to set the world ablaze with holy desire. Help me not to fear the heat of that divine fire. Crucify my lusts and resurrect my deepest erotic yearnings so that I might seek only what is true, good, and beautiful. Show me your perfect eros-agape love so that I might turn from my idols and find myself rejoicing in the wine of your salvation. Amen.

Part II

When the
"Language of the Body"
Becomes the
Language of the Liturgy

Chapter 7

Conjugal Life and Liturgical Life

Matt and Rose had been married for twenty-two years. Their relationship was cordial and decent, but they had fallen into some bad habits. As one of many symptoms, their sex life had become, well, perfunctory. The pattern had been the same for years. Once or twice a week, Matt would make his desire known and Rose knew what to expect from then on. They would crawl into bed, Matt would have his pleasure, and when it was over – longing to feel connected, longing to feel loved and cherished – Rose would feel lonelier than ever. The unanswered yearning of her heart was a silent pain that she carried. And it was becoming unbearable.

Communication skills they learned at a Marriage Encounter Weekend enabled Rose at long last to broach the topic with Matt. He listened, and while at first he was pretty defensive, the lines of communication began to open up. Over several months they had many long, sometimes painful, conversations about their lack of true intimacy.

When they sought the advice of a trusted priest, he casually asked them if they ever prayed together. Oh they said grace before meals and an occasional Our Father or Hail Mary together, if something warranted a quick prayer. But nothing beyond that. "My gift to you," Father Schilling said, "if you're open to it, is to teach you how to pray together." They didn't really know what this had to do with their sex life, but since Father assured them it would help, they agreed to try.

As we mentioned previously, John Paul observes that it is as if the spouses from the Song lived and expressed themselves in an ideal world in which the struggle between good and evil, love and lust, did not exist (see TOB 115:2). It is essential to have that ideal revealed to us, to let us know what God truly desires for us and what we should be aiming for. The love revealed in the Song of Songs is not unattainable. But we must be willing to *fight* for it. And we must be convinced that it is worth fighting for. Otherwise we will throw in the towel and settle for less.

The marriage of Tobias and Sarah in the book of Tobit reveals just what's at stake and how fierce the battle can be. Their marriage reveals, as John Paul will show us (we will examine this beginning in the next chapter), that the only path to victory is to allow erotic love to be taken up into the mystery and power of the Church's liturgy. Conjugal life must become, and is meant in some way to be, *liturgical*.

These reflections bring us to the peak of John Paul's dramatic proposal about the "greatness" – the God-likeness – of spousal love as a sacramental sign. Here we cross the threshold and enter into the most profound integration of the sexual and the sacred. But before we turn directly to the Pope's reflections, we must understand correctly what "liturgy" is. Precisely because of the profound link between spousal love and the liturgy, a failure to understand one leads to a failure to understand the other. Sadly, as Cardinal Ratzinger stated plainly, "liturgical education today, of both priests and laity, is deficient to a deplorable extent" (SL, p. 175). We have all but lost a sense of what the liturgy is, of what it is meant to be, and of what it accomplishes in those who enter into its "great mystery." Why? In large part because we have lost a sense of what marriage is, of what it is meant to be, and of what it accomplishes in those who enter into its "great mystery."

As mentioned in the Introduction, the liturgical chaos of the last several decades seems inextricably linked with the sexual chaos of the same period. I would even go so far as to say that the Second Vatican Council's promise of liturgical renewal was, at the same time, a prophecy of the renewal of marriage and family life. For you cannot have one (liturgical renewal) without the other (renewal of marriage and family life). Of course, we have yet to see either, but I am convinced that John Paul's TOB will play a critical role in both.

The "Great Mystery" of Liturgy

In Christian tradition, liturgy "means the participation of the People of God in 'the work of God'" (CCC 1069). The work of God refers above all to the "great mystery" of our redemption in Jesus Christ accomplished through his death and resurrection. The "transforming power of God," Cardinal Ratzinger tells us, is what "makes the liturgy what it is." God "wants, through what happens in the liturgy, to transform us and the world" (SL, p. 175).

To say that conjugal life is liturgical is to say that it participates in the "great mystery" of transforming the universe. As such, the union of man and woman in conjugal love is meant to sanctify the world as a living sign of redemption — a constant reminder of what happened in the death and resurrection of Christ. "It is this mystery of Christ that the Church proclaims and celebrates in her liturgy so that the faithful may live from it and bear witness to it in the world" (CCC 1068). Spouses do precisely this when they live in fidelity to the language God inscribed in their bodies as male and female. As John Paul II wrote, "Spouses are therefore the permanent reminder to the Church of what happened on the Cross" (FC 13). How so? What happened on the Cross, as various mystics describe it, was the consummation of a marriage – the mystical marriage of Christ and the Church. Spouses, in and through the language of their bodies, are to "enter into" this mystery, become a living icon of it, and proclaim it to the whole world. And only the *liturgy* provides entrance into this "great mystery."

Worshiping God with Our Bodies

The *Catechism* also says that liturgy is the Church's "celebration of divine worship" (1070). In fact, it is "a participation in Christ's own prayer addressed to the Father in the Holy Spirit" (1073). And what is prayer? Pope Benedict XVI, drawing on the teaching of the Church Fathers, says that "prayer, properly understood, is nothing other than becoming a longing for God" (MCS, p. 15). So, too, is conjugal life. When lived according to the "great mystery" of God's designs, even the marital embrace itself becomes a profound prayer, a profound *longing for God*. It becomes "eucharistic" as an act of thanksgiving offered to God for the joyous gift of sharing in his life and love. If, in the language of St. Augustine, the Cross can be considered a "marriage bed," conversely, according to the analogy, we might also view the marriage bed as an "altar" upon which spouses offer their bodies in living sacrifice, holy and acceptable to God. This is their spiritual act of worship (see Rom 12:1). This is precisely the goal of the liturgy, according to Pope Benedict, "that 'our bodies' (that is, our bodily existence on earth) become a 'living sacrifice,' united to the Sacrifice of Christ" (SL, p. 58).

For the Christian, worshiping God "in spirit and truth" (Jn 4:23) cannot possibly mean leaving our bodies behind. In the liturgy, Christ "offers himself to us [and to his Father] in his Body and Blood, and thus in a corporeal way" (SL, p. 175). We, too, must offer our bodies to the Lord and to one another. This is precisely what spouses are meant to do whenever they become "one flesh." They are meant to be uniting their "holy communion" with the Holy Communion of Christ and the Church in such a profound "communion of communions" that the two communions — that of husband and wife and that of Christ and the Church — form *one* great sign, *one* great sacrament, *one* act of worship, *one* great liturgical mystery (see TOB 95b:7).

We worship that which we think will satisfy our deepest hunger. In his first commandment, then — "You shall have no other gods before me ..." (Dt 5:7) — God is simply saying: "I am your satisfaction; I, and I alone, can satisfy your hunger." As the psalmist puts it, "You shall not bow down to a foreign god. I am the Lord your God ... Open your mouth wide, and I will fill it" (Ps 81:9-10). Our world worships the body, worships sex. Why? Because so many of us have come to believe that sexual union will satisfy our deepest hunger. The world is on to something here. For marital union *is* meant to be an *icon* of our ultimate satisfaction. It's meant to point us to Christ. But when we worship the paint and the wood of a religious icon rather than letting it open a window to heaven, we stop short (far short!) of what we truly desire and the icon degenerates into an idol.

Isn't this what Christ is helping the thirsty Samaritan woman to understand? She had been trying to satisfy her thirst with six men, six being the imperfect biblical number. Jesus comes to her as her "seventh husband" – the perfect biblical number. Jesus presents himself to her as her perfect satisfaction. In his dialogue with her, it is as if he were saying: "I know you are thirsty for love, I know. But, my dearly beloved, you have been 'looking for love in all the wrong places ... looking for love in too many faces.' *I'm the love you've been looking for!* If you only knew the gift of God ... if you only knew the love that *I* wanted to give you ... You would ask, and I would give it to you ... and you would never thirst again. In fact, this love will well up in you to eternal life" (see Jn 4:10-14). That day, having found the "living water" of Christ, the Samaritan woman became a "true worshiper" (Jn 4:23). When we find that which truly satisfies our thirst and vulnerably surrender ourselves to it, then we are worshiping God "in spirit and in truth."

In short, the Christian revolution transforms sexual union from something that is *worshiped* into something that *is* worship. When lived sacramentally and liturgically, spouses are not seeking ultimate satisfaction in their union. Rather, they find in their union a sign, a foreshadowing, of ultimate satisfaction. And in that sign, through that sign, they offer praise and worship *to God* with a living hope in the consummation of the Marriage of the Lamb. It is union with God – participation in the eternal bliss of the divine exchange – that alone satisfies the heart's thirst.

Liturgy as Proclamation and Love

Liturgy also refers "to the proclamation of the Gospel and to active charity" carried out by the Church "in the image of her Lord" (CCC 1070). So does conjugal life. Conjugal life is a profound and continuous proclamation of the "Gospel of the body" lived in the image of Christ's love for the Church. Quoting from the Second Vatican Council, the *Catechism* concludes: "The liturgy then is rightly seen as an exercise of the priestly office of Jesus Christ. It involves the presentation of man's sanctification under the guise of signs perceptible by the senses and its accomplishment in ways appropriate to each of these signs" (1070). In conjugal life, the sanctification of spouses is presented and appropriately accomplished through the sign of their faithful union, lived out day by day and consummated in becoming one flesh.

Pope Benedict XVI says that, through the liturgy, God "makes himself accessible to us, so that, through the things of the earth, through our gifts, we can communicate with him in a personal way" (SL, p. 173). We can say the same thing about marriage in its liturgical dimension: God makes himself accessible to spouses through their earthly gift of married love, so that they can communicate with him — that is, enter into communion with God — in a personal way. Of course, as John Paul wrote, "All married life is a gift" (LF 12). This means every diaper change, every commute to the workplace, every birthday card given to one's spouse is part of the every day "liturgy" of married life. But just as the Church's liturgy reaches its summit in the bodily offering of the Eucharist, so too does the liturgical giving of married life become "most evident when the spouses, in giving themselves to each other in love, bring about that encounter which makes them 'one flesh'" (LF 12).

The idea that conjugal life is liturgical is not surprising when we consider that the whole liturgical life of the Church revolves around the sacraments (see CCC 1113). And marriage is not only one of the sacraments. According to the Holy Father, marriage is in some sense the prototype or model of *all* the sacraments (see TOB 98:2). For the goal of all the sacraments is to unite the Church with her Bridegroom and to fill her – or, in keeping with the analogy, "impregnate" her – with divine life. John Paul thus concludes that marriage, inasmuch as it is linked to the "great mystery" of Christ and of the Church, is *"the foundation of the whole sacramental order"* (TOB 95b:7). In other words, that order by which God makes his invisible mystery of love visible (the "sacramental order") is founded upon the original mystery of marriage. This, in fact, is the very purpose, the very reason for marriage in God's plan – to reveal and proclaim to the world the "great mystery" of Christ and his life-giving union with the Church (see Eph 5:31-32).

The Spousal Analogy Works in Two Directions

Marriage not only illuminates the "great mystery" of Christ and the Church, but Christ's union with the Church shines definitive light on marriage. When we read the spousal analogy from the other direction – that is, beginning with Christ's relationship with the Church and then moving to husband and wife – we realize that "marriage, in its deepest essence, *emerges from the mystery* of God's eternal love for ... humanity" (TOB 90:4). As John Paul asserts, this means "that marriage corresponds to the vocation of Christians only when it mirrors the love that Christ, the Bridegroom, gives to the Church, his Bride, and which the Church ... seeks to give back to Christ in return. This is the redeeming, saving love, the love with which man has been loved by God from eternity in Christ" (TOB 90:2).

This means marital love is quite a lofty calling. It is meant to save us from sin and death and prepare us for heaven. Who by his own strength can live this divine love? Only the grace of salvation makes it possible. And this is precisely what the Church's liturgical life offers us. This is why marital love, if it is to be truly itself, must be "liturgical." Marital love must constantly draw life from the mystery of the Church's liturgy – that is, from the Church's ongoing *entering into* union with Christ. If it does not, spouses will have no "wine" with which to fulfill their vocation.

The love of husband and wife (consummated when the two become "one flesh") and the love of Christ and the Church (consummated sacramentally in the Eucharist) are so intimately related, according to Ephesians 5, as to form one "great mystery," a *single great sacrament* (see TOB 95b:7). Hence, not only is conjugal life liturgical. When we read the spousal analogy in the other direction, we realize that the Church's liturgical life is also "conjugal" – it involves the union of spouses: Christ and the Church.

In this section of his teaching, John Paul wants to unfold how the "language of the body" is founded on the language of the liturgy. However, in the course of his reflections, he will also demonstrate that the language of the liturgy is *modeled after the "language of the body"* (see TOB 117:6). The key, as we shall see more clearly, to entering deeply into the Church's liturgy is to realize the liturgy's "spousal" nature. The goal of all liturgy is the union of the Bridegroom and the Bride, Christ and his Church.

Much is at stake in this "great mystery" of spousal union – both that of husband and wife and that of Christ and the Church. As we will see in the next chapter, the Old Testament story of Tobias and Sarah demonstrates that living marital love "liturgically" is quite literally a matter of life and death. There is an enemy who has been hell-bent right from the beginning on writing *lust and death* into God's plan of *love and life*. Tobias and Sarah demonstrate that living marital union as "liturgy" is the only way to assure victory over this fierce enemy.

Father Schilling was well versed in John Paul II's TOB, and he liked to talk in spousal categories, especially when he was working with couples. "Prayer," he taught them, "is getting spiritually naked before God. It's where, with the certainty of God's love, we remove all of our masks, all of our 'fig leaves,' and let God's light shine on our real humanity – warts and all. As we persevere, God's light dispels the darkness and the shadows in our lives. Lack of intimacy," he told them, "whether with God or your spouse, or anyone else, usually means we're hiding in the shadows, we're hiding behind some kind of fig leaf. We're afraid we won't be loved in our nakedness, so, just like Adam and Eve, we hide."

Both Matt and Rose listened intently. His words were hitting home. "There's nothing more intimate in our relationship with God than knowing that we are loved by him in our nakedness. That kind of intimacy with God, that kind of prayer," Father assured them, "is what prepares you for real intimacy with one another, and real intimacy with one another is what prepares you for a truly fulfilling sex life. Praying together as spouses," he said, "means together exposing all that your marriage is to God – the good, the bad, and the ugly – so he can love you there, teach you to love one another there, and enter the journey of healing." Father paused and leaned forward. Then came the shocker: "Have you ever invited God into your marriage bed?" he asked. "He wants to be part of the action."

Rose had never thought to do that, but something in her heart leapt when Father suggested it. Matt, on the other hand, was dumbfounded. God and sex didn't seem to go together in his mind. "Try it," Father Schilling said in a tone of voice that implied "trust me, I've seen this transform other marriages and I know what I'm talking about." "What do you have to lose?"

Matt quipped, "What are you saying, that we're supposed to get on our knees before sex and say, 'Bless us, O Lord, and these thy gifts which we are about to receive ...'?" Father chimed in: "Actually, that's not a bad place to start. But the point is not to add a prayer 'on top' of what you're doing. The goal is to turn your nakedness and union with each other *into a prayer*, into an experience of nakedness and union before God, with God." It seemed more than a little strange at first, but following Father Schilling's advice, in their own awkward way, they started offering their whole relationship to God when they offered their whole selves to each other in their marital union.

Four years later, the idea that marital love is something "liturgical" is not just an idea. It has become more and more a lived experience for them. Old habits have a way of sneaking back in on occasion and old pains can resurface, but Matt and Rose now have a profoundly effective way of working through those hurts and pains – by uniting their union with the sacrifice of Christ, exposing all that they are to his healing light.

Reflection Questions

I. What is your initial reaction to the idea that marital love and union is meant to be something "liturgical," an act of prayer and worship?

2. "Keep God out of the bedroom" is a common sentiment. Where does this come from? Why is it so difficult for many people to imagine God wanting to be an intimate part of the marital act? If it is difficult for me to imagine it, what steps can I take to begin healing?

Suggested Prayer

(*For married people*) Lord, thank you for the gift of my spouse. You know everything about us and our relationship, all our pains and fears and hopes and longings. You know all the obstacles in our hearts to true intimacy. Teach us how to open everything that we are to you when we come together in our marital embrace. We want to open our union more deeply to your presence. Teach us how. Send your fire upon us so that we might learn how to sing the Song of Songs in our union without fear, without hesitancy, without shame. Transform our union into praise of you. Amen.

(For unmarried people) Lord, you have placed within me a deep longing for union. Help me to realize that that longing is really a cry of my heart for you, that that longing is really a prayer. Show me how to live all of my longings and desires as prayer. Help me to see that you, and you alone are able to satisfy the ache of my heart. Amen.

Chapter 8

The Marriage of Tobias and Sarah

Tim and Teresa had suffered everything imaginable in their marriage. Tim was addicted to pornography and masturbation. Teresa was addicted to gambling and shopping. Between the two of them, their addictions had put the family nearly $75,000 in debt. When it came out in the open that both of them were having affairs, they told their children that they were getting a divorce.

Their parish priest got news of their impending plans and invited them to his office. He began their meeting with a simple question: "Do you know why God created marriage?" Tim looked at Teresa and both shrugged their shoulders. "No, not really," Tim muttered. "What do you mean?" "Well, before you seek to end your marriage, don't you think you should first know what your marriage is for?" They never really thought their marriage had some big "purpose" from God. They got married, like everybody else, with hopes of happiness, and since their marriage was delivering anything but, they wanted out. By the end of their meeting, Tim and Teresa had agreed to postpone their plans to divorce for one month, during which time they would study the *Catechism of the Catholic Church*'s teaching on marriage.

Twelve years later, Tim and Teresa are now both active in their parish's marriage ministry, helping to prepare couples for marriage and to save existing marriages from divorce.

We read in the book of Tobit that, before marrying Tobias, Sarah had already married seven others. But through the work of the demon Asmodeus, each man died in the bridal chamber on his wedding night before consummating the marriage (see Tobit 6:13–14). (Talk about an anti-climactic honeymoon!)

Now let's place ourselves in Tobias' shoes. The angel Raphael tells Tobias that he is to marry Sarah. John Paul II – man of keen insight that he is – observes that Tobias *had reason to be afraid!* (see TOB 114:5). In fact, Sarah's father was so convinced of Tobias' imminent death that on the wedding day he was already digging Tobias' grave (see Tobit 8:9).

If, at first, Tobias was understandably reluctant to take Sarah as his wife, it was the angel Raphael who changed his mind. "Now listen to me, brother," says Raphael to Tobias, "for she will become your wife; and do not worry about the demon, for this very night she will be given to you in marriage ... Do not be afraid, for she was destined for you from eternity. You will save her, and she will go with you, and ... you will have children by her." Then we read: "When Tobias heard these things, he fell in love with her and yearned deeply for her" (Tobit 6:15, 17).

Love as a Test of Life-or-Death

Here we see all the components of good and evil gearing up for a great spiritual battle: angels and demons; life and death; God's eternal saving will and man's fearful resistance; love and all that is opposed to love. How can the spouses overcome the demon, conquer death, cast out fear, and enter into God's saving plan so that love and life triumph? *Only by entering into the "great mystery" of liturgy* — of man's union with God.

And in what context does this great clash, this decisive battle, occur? As John Paul says, "Everything, in fact, happens during the couple's wedding night" (TOB 114:8). Just as the "great mystery" centers on a man and woman joining in "one flesh" (see Eph 5) so does the "great battle" (see Eph 6). Precisely in this "conjugal union," John Paul tells us, "the choices and acts [of the spouses] take on the whole weight of human existence" (TOB 115:3).

"Whoa! Hold on! Can't sex just be fun? Why does it have to be so heavy?" Well, the fact is that human life, human existence, *is* heavy. Contrary to the modern world's treatment of it, sex is not a light matter. It is not entertainment. Sex is something *existential* — that is, it concerns the very reality and foundations of human existence, of human life. And "all of human life," as the Second Vatican Council observed, "shows itself to be a dramatic struggle between good and evil, between light and darkness" (GS 13). In fact, the union of husband and wife "is placed at the center of the great struggle between good and evil, between life and death, between love and all that is opposed to love" (LF 23).

It is no coincidence that St. Paul follows his presentation of the "great mystery" of spousal union in Ephesians 5 with a call to take up arms in the cosmic struggle between good and evil in Ephesians 6. We see here, as John Paul expresses, that when spouses "unite as husband and wife, they must find themselves in the situation in which *the powers of good and evil fight against each other*" (TOB 115:2). Husbands and wives live this great *spiritual* contest in their *bodies*. We see this vividly in the case of Tobias and Sarah. From the first moment of their marriage, their love had *to face the test of life-or-death.* "The words about love 'strong as death,' spoken by the spouses of the Song of Songs ... here take on the character of a real test" (TOB 114:6).

In acknowledging this "heaviness," we should also remember that we spoke about discovering an eros that has launched beyond earth's gravitational pull and into weightless freedom (chapter 3). Paradoxically, we experience this *weightlessness* only to the degree that we embrace the real *weight* of the Cross. In deep union/intimacy with Christ, we discover that, although he carried the weight of the world on his shoulders, Christ's "yoke is easy" and his "burden is light" (Mt 11:30). It's only to the degree that we resist the weight of the Cross that it becomes a crushing burden.

The Ecstasy and Agony of Becoming "One Flesh"

In the Song of Songs, we saw the spouses rereading the true "language" of their bodies through an ongoing loving dialogue of heartfelt sentiment, affection, and erotic longing. We saw also how eros (sexual love) overcomes its own limits by opening to apape (divine love). In Tobit, by contrast, "the distressing situation of the 'limit' together with the test of life-or-death brings *the loving dialogue of the spouses in some way to silence*" (TOB 115:3). If the Song of Songs reveals the *ecstasy* of becoming one flesh, the marriage of Tobias and Sarah reveals the *agony*. Only by holding the two together do we get a realistic vision of marriage.

Catholic writer Melinda Selmys brought this point out well in an article entitled "Divorce: In the Image and Likeness of Hell" (*National*

Catholic Register, Sept. 30, 2007). The first few sentences confirmed what I intuited from the title – Selmys was going to speak plainly. It seems she'd had enough of the sweet, pious lingo with which many Catholic writers often speak about marriage (heck, for all I know, she may have had me in mind). She observes, "The theologians remind us that our married life is an image of the union between ... Christ [and the Church]. We hear of ... the bliss of the two becoming one." When things get tough, we are told "to improve our communication, fall in love with each other all over again, observe the tender moments, etc., etc."

Then she allows such advice to butt up against the all-too-real experiences of actual marriages. "But how are you to fall in love again," she asks, "with an insensitive beast who has broken your heart and slept with another woman? How can you see your sex life as an image of the intimate life of the blessed Trinity when your wife consents only on a full moon when Mars is in Virgo, and makes love with the enthusiasm of a dead frog?" I didn't know whether to laugh or cry the first time I read that last line. For whatever reason, such brutally honest writing seems rare in much of the Catholic press. It is as if those who promote Catholic teaching are afraid it will not go over so well if we talk about the real sufferings of following Jesus. So we conveniently promote the glories of the Christian life without a realistic assessment of the sorrows. I, myself, have probably been guilty of that on occasion.

Marriage is a messy, painful business. If spouses are to love as Christ loves, how could it be otherwise? Christ's marriage is consummated *through his passion and death*. This means, as Selmy observes, that marriage will involve "the same agony, the mingling of tears and blood, the same thorns digging into our skulls, the same nails plowed through our palms." Because so many people believe the Church is "down on sex," the glories and ecstasies to which authentic Catholic teaching calls spouses (as exemplified in the Song of Songs) *should* be emphasized. But these glories and ecstasies are the fruit of embracing *much* purifying suffering (as exemplified in the marriage of Tobias and Sarah). If the joy is not set before us, we will have no motivation to endure the suffering. "For the joy set before him Christ endured the Cross" (Heb 12:2). But if the path to those joys is not also realistically assessed, we will naively wonder why marriage can be so difficult, even agonizing.

But let me clarify something important about the "agony" involved in following Christ. It is sweet. St. Louis de Montfort says that, as we give ourselves over entirely to Christ through Mary, Mary dips all of our crosses "in the honey of her maternal sweetness." Then we can readily swallow our crosses as we would "sugared almonds" (TD 154). The point is this: there is a beautiful consolation granted those who are united with Christ on the Cross. For even in the midst of his agonizing cry, "My God, my God, why have you abandoned me!?" (Mt 27:46), Christ remained mysteriously consoled in the loving embrace of the Father.

As a priest friend of mine expresses it, when united with Christ, all sorrow is a consolation and a movement of grace, a gift of God. However, without faith that God is loving us and choosing to be with us *in our broken-heartedness*, our sufferings lock us in a self-enclosed prison. Love inevitably involves the Cross. But it doesn't depend on us to love as we are called to love. We must humbly depend on Christ to love *in us* and *through us*, to suffer *in us* and *through us*. Our "loud cries and tears" then become "prayer and supplication" offered to Abba (Heb 5:7). And strangely enough, because we *know* that in these sufferings we are united with Christ, there is no place we would rather be. We are consoled. The suffering is sweet.

The Body's Final Word

We see this mysterious simultaneity of bliss and pain by considering the lovers of the Song together with Tobias and Sarah. In the Song of Songs, the spouses experience an intense mutual fascination and a deep pleasure in reading the language of their bodies. In Tobit, Tobias and Sarah soberly recognize that "the touchstone of a test of life-or-death [is] also part of the 'language of the body'" (TOB 115:3). They realize in their call to union that "the body expresses itself also through *the mystery of life and death*. It expresses itself through this mystery more eloquently perhaps than ever" (TOB 115:3).

Isn't "death," in fact, the final word our bodies speak on this earth? Few couples are thinking about this distressing fact on the day of their wedding – indeed, it is usually the furthest thing from a bride and groom's mind (although, if the couple were to look at their wedding's liturgical setting, they would observe that they are pledging themselves *unto death* underneath the corpus of a crucified Bridegroom and right in front of an altar of sacrifice). Tobias and Sarah had to stare this distressing word "death" in the face right from the outset of their marriage. "What depth does their love acquire in this way ... ?" asks John Paul (TOB 115:3). And we might also ask, what depth does their love *require* if they are to stare death in the face and overcome it?

As Christians, we know, in fact, that "death" is *not* the final word of the body. For Christ's death is the precursor to his bodily *resurrection* and *ascension* into heavenly glory. How can spouses possibly enter into *this* truth of the body and thus be saved from the inevitable finality of death? Only through the prayer and mystery of the liturgy. As Pope Benedict says, in the liturgy a "demand is made on the body in all its involvement in the circumstances of everyday life. The body is required to become 'capable of resurrection,' to orient itself toward the resurrection, toward the Kingdom of God" (SL, p. 176).

How can our bodies possibly become "capable of resurrection"? How can we orient ourselves toward the resurrection? By orienting ourselves toward Calvary: "For if we have been united with him in a death like his, we shall certainly be united with him in a resurrection like his" (Rom 6:5). All of this happens by entering into the "great mystery" of the Church's liturgy. *That* is the doorway that allows us access to Christ's saving death and resurrection. Liturgy is where the saving death and resurrection of Christ is re-presented to and received by the human heart.

The Prayer of Tobias and Sarah

Tobias knows that if he is to conquer death through love, he must be mindful of Raphael's instructions. The angel had given him various pieces of advice on how to free himself from the demon's grip. Above all, however, Raphael recommended prayer (see TOB 114:7): "When you enter the bridal chamber," the angel had said, "when you approach her, rise up, both of you, and cry out to the merciful God, and he will save you and have mercy on you" (Tobit 6:16-17).

"With this promise," John Paul says, "it was easier for both to face the test of life-or-death awaiting them on the wedding night" (TOB 114:8). In the book of Tobit we find neither a dialogue nor a duet between the spouses, as with the lovers in the Song of Songs. Instead, as

John Paul observes, Tobias and Sarah "decide above all *to speak in unison* — and this unison is nothing other than prayer. In that unison ... man and woman are united not only through the communion of hearts, but also through the union of both in facing the great test" (TOB 115:4).

Nothing solidifies spousal union more than the shared experiences of deep, intimate prayer coupled with a common goal of facing *and overcoming* — with the help of God's grace — great trials. Tobias and Sarah witness to the fact that there is no trial in married life — *not even the prospect of death!* — that prayer cannot overcome. Tobias and Sarah's prayer "becomes the one and only word in virtue of which the new spouses meet the test" (TOB 115:5). As we read in Tobit:

> When the door was shut and the two were alone, Tobias got up from the bed and said, "Sister, get up, and let us pray that the Lord may have mercy upon us." And Tobias began to pray, "Blessed are you, O God of our fathers, and blessed be your holy and glorious name forever. Let the heavens and the whole creation bless you. You made Adam and gave him Eve his wife as a helper and support. From them the race of mankind has sprung. You said, 'It is not good that the man should be alone; let us make a helper for him like himself.'And now, O Lord, I am not taking this sister of mine because of lust, but with sincerity. Grant that I may find mercy and grow old together with her." And she said with him, "Amen." (Tobit 8:4–8)

Tobias and Sarah's prayer immerses itself in all the themes

that John Paul reflects on at great length in his TOB. The Pope's entire teaching is based on Christ's call to reflect on God's plan for marriage "in the beginning" (see Mt 19:8). Notice that this is just what Tobias and Sarah do. Notice that Tobias calls her "sister" like the bridegroom in the Song of Songs. Notice that he contrasts lust with the "sincere gift of self." Notice that he has "set her as a seal on his heart," for he intends to spend his whole life with her ("What therefore God has joined together let no man put asunder," Mt 19:6). And, perhaps most importantly, notice that Tobias knows they cannot live this sublime calling by relying on their own strength. They need God's mercy deeply; they need God's grace to *empower* them to overcome the *diabolic plan* of lust and death and live the *divine plan* of love and life. This is precisely what John Paul teaches throughout his TOB. Spouses cannot live their sexual union truthfully *"except through the powers that come ... from the Holy Spirit* who purifies, enlivens, strengthens, and perfects the powers of the human spirit" (TOB 131:3).

John Paul observes that in their prayer, Tobias and Sarah outline *the dimension of the liturgy* against the horizon of the "language of the body" (see TOB 114:8). Their prayer itself is an entering into the liturgy – an entering into the worship of God and their own sanctification. And it is all a preparation for their joining in "one flesh."

A Good or Bad Lot in Life

Much is riding on the disposition of Tobias and Sarah's hearts in this dramatic moment. The prospect of choosing between *love* and *lust* presents them with a test of good and evil, life and death – and not only in some abstract way. Their actions in this moment will determine whether they experience "a good or bad lot – in the dimension of life as a whole" (TOB 115:5).

There is a deep, hidden wisdom emanating here from John Paul II. He is taking us *to the root* of the modern crisis in marriage and family life. He is taking us *to the root* of the tensions and difficulties found in every marriage since the fall of man. And he is laying out the one and only necessary path for living marriage as God intended: somehow, men and women must find a way to *reverse the effects of the fall*, so to speak, and begin reclaiming deep within their hearts the purity of love as it was in the beginning. That "somehow" is by entering deeply into the liturgy, for liturgy is where the redemptive work of Christ reaches human hearts to heal and transform them. In and through the Church's liturgy, "Christ ... *opens* marriage to the salvific action of God, *to the powers flowing 'from the redemption of the body,'* which help to overcome the consequences of sin and to build the unity of man and woman according to the Creator's eternal plan" (TOB 100:2).

If we do not "enter into" the mystery of the liturgy expecting in faith to receive what we need, we are left to contend with the overwhelming powers of sin and lust on our own, and the result will be, to put it mildly, a "bad lot" in life. So few married people (and men and women in general) seem to understand the far-reaching consequences of their sexual choices and, even more, of the disposition of heart with which they approach sexual union. These serve as a barometer, of sorts, that can measure and predict "a good or bad lot" in the whole of their life together. Indeed, one would be hard-pressed to find any marital difficulty that cannot be traced, directly or indirectly, to a failure to read the language of the body truthfully.

The true language of the body calls us to a mutually naked – not just physically! – gift of person to person in which each is received unconditionally by the other as he or she really is. This is intimacy in the marriage bed as it was meant to be. To the degree that we are "hiding" – and physical nakedness is no guarantee that we have removed our "fig leaves" – we fail to read the language of the body truthfully and, at least to some degree, fail to realize a true union of persons. I say "to some degree" because, as any married couple knows, the full revelation of your inner self to your spouse is a journey, a life-long journey of growing in trust and self-discovery. Obviously, a couple who have been married for decades will be able to reach a level of "in-to-me-see" in their union that newlyweds won't. That doesn't mean that the newlyweds are necessarily "hiding" from each other or failing to experience a real union of their persons. It just means that intimacy in the marital embrace grows and matures with time. But that growth is not easy; and it's certainly not automatic. In fact, the real internal difficulty of realizing a true and lasting union of persons in each particular sexual act is, according to John Paul II, "the internal problem of every marriage" (LR p. 225).

Every marriage is a struggle to overcome the effects of sin on the human heart and to love as God intended in the beginning. And *every* marriage fails in numerous ways to do so. But for all our failures in this regard, for all our miseries, hope is not lost. We, like Tobias and Sarah, can follow the archangel Raphael's instructions and enter into the mystery and power of liturgical prayer. We, like Tobias and Sarah, can always cry out for mercy. Liturgy, in fact, is always an encounter with the Father who is rich in mercy. The Latin for mercy, *misericordia*, actually means "a heart that gives itself to those in misery." God is not repulsed by our miseries – he is drawn to them! And he yearns to free our hearts from all miseries, great and small so that we can be free to love in his image.

Love is Victorious Because it Prays

Tobias and Sarah realize that there is a demon actively seeking to thwart their love, to wreak havoc, to strike them with suffering and death. "But *in order to repel the evil* threatening to kill the body," and this is one of John Paul's key points, "one must *prevent the evil spirit from having access to the soul*, one must free oneself within oneself from his influence" (TOB 115:5).

This demonic influence goes right back to "the beginning," when the first man and woman exchanged the truth of God for a lie and the original plan of sexual love degenerated into sexual lust. At that moment, eros was cut off from agape, and, ever since, men and women have struggled to express the true "spousal meaning" of their bodies. Ever since, men and women have struggled to hold God and sex together. But, again, let us not forget the good news! If lust causes many "errors" in reading the true language of the body, through the gift of redemption there is always the possibility of passing from error to truth, the possibility of conversion through life in the Holy Spirit (see TOB 107:3).

The demon's influence is death-dealing, as Sarah and her seven previous husbands discovered quite dramatically. And the demon's goal, it seems, is to separate eros from agape. But Tobias' love for Sarah is not a diseased form of eros. Tobias' passion for Sarah (he "yearned deeply for her," Tobit 6:17) is imbued with the fire of agape. Tobias' prayer, as a liturgical reality, reveals the true desire of his heart to love her rightly: to love her as God loves. And relying totally on God's mercy, their prayer enables the newly wed spouses to be confident in love's victory.

It enables them to "go without hesitating toward this... test of life-or-death." And in this test "*life has the victory*, because, during the test of the first wedding night, *love supported by prayer is revealed as stronger than death*." Love "is victorious because it prays" (TOB, pp. 597, 601).

From within the bridal chamber, Tobias and Sarah transform the "language of the body" into a single voice of prayer – "And Sarah said with him, 'Amen'" (Tobit 8:8). This voice, this act of praying in unison "allows both of them to pass beyond the 'limit situation' [recall the 'limits' of eros from chapter 6], beyond the threat of evil and death, inasmuch as they open themselves totally, in the unity of the two, to the living God" (TOB 115:6). *This* is the key point: if spouses are to overcome lust and the certainty of death that comes with it (see Rom 8:6), they must open their union totally to the presence of the living God, to the "Lord and Giver of Life." This is the "Word" written by God into the language of the body: *life!* But as we see from the first pages of Genesis and confirmed here in the book of Tobit, there is a meddling force at work, an "anti-Word" who wants to write "death" into this language.

"Do not worry about the demon," says St. Raphael (Tobit 6:15). Why shouldn't Tobias and Sarah worry? They had every reason to expect the worst. Why shouldn't they be afraid? Because as St. John tells us: "There is no fear in love, but perfect love casts out fear" (1 Jn 4:18). The "perfect love" that casts out Tobias and Sarah's fear, however, is not their own. Their love for each other, like that of every couple, is riddled with imperfections. But through their prayer, they have opened to a perfect love that does not originate in them: they have opened to God's love, which has been poured into their hearts through the Holy Spirit who has been given to them (see Rom 5:5).

In a clarion call for all men and women to embrace this perfect love — almost repeating his signature phrase "be not afraid" — John Paul declares: "The truth and the strength of love show themselves in the ability to place oneself between the forces of good and of evil that fight within man and around him, because love is confident in the victory of good and is ready to do everything in order that good may conquer" (TOB 115:2). No sacrifice is too great for true lovers — no suffering too much to bear — when it is needed to ensure the victory of good over evil, love over lust, life over death.

This is precisely the testimony of the Cross, of Christ's spousal love for the Church. This is precisely the perfect love in which every husband and wife are called to participate. The good news is that by "following Christ, renouncing themselves, and taking up their crosses ...spouses will be able to 'receive' the original meaning of marriage and live it with the help of Christ" (CCC 1615). With Christ's help, all spouses, like Tobias and Sarah, can overcome the work of the "demon of lust and death" and live according to the "Spirit of love and life." And, as we shall see in the next chapter, all of this is contained in what the Pope calls the "conjugal creed."

Postponing their divorce and reading about God's plan for marriage in the *Catechism* stirred a hunger in Tim and Teresa to want to learn more. They started reading every book they could get their hands on that talked about God's plan for marriage and how to make it work. A key breakthrough for Tim was understanding that when marriage exposes a person's selfishness and sins it's doing what it is *meant* to do: bringing our sins and wounds to light so we can recognize them, confess them, and begin the healing process.

"Our healing process," says Tim, "has been long and painful. We've had layers and layers of sins and wounds and fears to work through, and even though we've come a long way, we both know there's still more to look at. All in God's timing." Teresa says, "We had to learn how to love and trust each other all over again. At times it's been like open-heart surgery without anesthesia."

A major stumbling block along the way of their healing was the Church's teaching on permanent "openness to life" in sexual intercourse. Teresa had had her tubes tied during her second C-section. The contradiction in their "whole hearted" enthusiasm for everything the Church taught about marriage — *except* this — was looming large.*

I first met Tim at a men's retreat at which I was speaking. He admits that when I got to the podium he was skeptical: *What could this young guy [I was 29 at the time] possibly teach me about being a man,* he thought to himself. Of course, I can't take credit for what God did in Tim's heart that day, but he was deeply convicted that his wife's sterilization — which he had forcefully

---

* If you are unconvinced about the Church's teaching regarding contraception, you are not alone. But for a few pockets here and there, there has been a void of good catechesis on the subject for at least two generations. People have generally heard the "what" of the Church's teaching, but rarely, if ever the "why." To learn more about this critical issue, visit One More Soul's website omsoul.com. You may also want to read my book *Good News About Sex and Marriage: Answers to Your Honest Questions about Catholic Teaching* which deals extensively with the subject.

encouraged — was the unsuspected root of a lot of pain and dysfunction in their relationship. He was overcome with a sense that they had opened themselves and their marriage to something very dark when he and Teresa had willfully closed her womb to life.

If the marriage bed is a "test of life and death," Tim was realizing that he and Teresa had chosen a kind of death. There *is* something dark at work, a meddling spirit that wants to write evil and death into the marriage bed. Spouses can save themselves from this threat, the Pope says, only "inasmuch as they open themselves totally, in the unity of the two, to the living God" (TOB 115:6). Both Tim and Teresa came to see that, so long as they were content with their decision to be sterilized, they were not "opening themselves totally to the living God." In fact, they were willfully shutting him out.

Having confessed their sterilization — and knowing that they weren't absolutely obligated to do so — Teresa underwent sterilization reversal surgery. They have had two more children since and are forever grateful for how these children have drawn their whole family closer together.

Reflection Questions

I. In what ways have I tasted "agony" in love? What have I done with those pains, sorrows, and sufferings? Have I felt imprisoned by them? Have I experienced the consolation of being united with Christ in them?

2. Do I believe that I am created for ecstasy, that God wants to fill me with his own ecstatic joy? In what ways have I tasted a holy "ecstasy" in love?

Suggested Prayer

Jesus, you promise that even though we experience sorrow now, our hearts will rejoice and no one will take our joy from us (see Jn 16:22). You promise that as we abide in your love and keep the Father's commandments, your joy will be in us and our joy will be complete (see Jn 15:9-11). Teach us how to abide in your love! Show us the pathway into your heart and teach us how to open all the hidden chambers of our hearts to you. Teach us how to keep the Father's commandments without fear, without hesitancy. Teach us how to embrace that mysterious blending of bliss and pain that unites us so intimately with you. Amen.

Chapter 9

The Spouses' "Conjugal Creed"

> Dan and Kris both went to a reputable Catholic university,
> well known for its theological orthodoxy. They actually met
> in a marriage and family class largely devoted to studying
> the teachings of John Paul II. They got engaged early in their
> senior year and married soon after graduation. Five years later,
> they were in a divorce court fighting bitterly over custody of
> their two children.

One of the high points of the Church's liturgy is the profession of her Creed. The Creed encompasses in just a few words all the knowledge contained in both the Old and New Testaments (see CCC 186). To say it with faith is to enter into communion with the Trinity and with the whole Church (see CCC 197). In other words, to say the Creed with faith is to enter into the "great mystery" of the marriage of divinity and humanity consummated in Christ.

When Tobias and Sarah express the language of the liturgy with the language of their bodies – that is, when they express the "great mystery" of God's spousal love for humanity with their own spousal love for each other – their prayer becomes a profession of what John Paul insightfully describes as their "conjugal creed" (see TOB 116:2). As we have seen, this conjugal creed encompasses in just a few words the whole truth of the Theology of the Body contained in both the

Old and New Testaments. This creed originates from the depth of *love* in the new spouses' hearts and expresses itself in the *life*-giving language of their bodies. As such, this creed serves as a precise antidote to the demon's plot to write *lust* into their hearts and *death* into their bodies.

Victory over Evil through the Conjugal Creed

It would be all too easy to remain content with a symbolic interpretation of the demonic attack on Tobias and Sarah's marriage. It is my firm belief that John Paul II wants, instead, to help men and women see precisely what they are up against when they enter the sacrament of Marriage. They are entering, knowingly or unknowingly, into a war zone – into a raging spiritual battle for the very soul of humanity (see Eph 5-6). It seems to me that John Paul's reflections on Tobias and Sarah's marriage take very seriously – and want us to take very seriously – the fact that there is a spiritual enemy who comes to steal, kill, and destroy the gift of human life (see Jn 10:10), and he does so precisely by spewing all his vile hatred at the "great mystery" of the one-flesh union.

The demon that attacked Tobias and Sarah is real, not figurative. And, truth be told, there are real demons after us, to keep us from the life and love God desires for us. But we needn't be afraid of demons. They, in fact, are afraid of us! They are afraid that we are going to discover who we really are – sons and daughters of the Father who bear the very image of God. So they are hell-bent on keeping us from our true identity. Demons attack where we, deep in our spirits, are not trusting in God's love for us, are not believing in our true identity. As the enemy of human nature, demons want us to feel bad about ourselves, to think ill of our own humanity, of our bodies, of our hearts, especially of our weaknesses. It is in this way, as we say in the St. Michael prayer, that they "prowl about the world seeking the ruin of souls." But let us take courage! For he who is in us is greater – much greater! – than he who prowls about the world (see 1 Jn 4:4). And let us cast ourselves mystically into Mary's womb. For there we are "delivered from all anxiety, fear, and scruples" and we are "safeguarded from all our enemies, the devil, the world and sin, which have never gained admittance there" (TD 264). Within Mary's womb, we may still hear the roars of the lion who seeks to devour us, but he has absolutely no access to this holy chamber. And Christ is there with us.

By turning to Christ in our weaknesses and opening them to him, we *"prevent the evil spirit from having access to the soul"* (TOB 115:5). But when we fall prey to our weaknesses and substitute lust for authentic spousal love, it is a clear indication that the enemy – knowingly or unknowingly – has gained access. Lust is the enemy of authentic marital love, and its bitter fruit is *death* and *destruction*: the death of love, the death of marriage, and the death of the family. In turn, when the cradle of life – the family – breeds death and destruction, it inevitably produces an entire "culture of death."

How, then, can spouses free themselves from the influence of the demons that threaten to destroy their love? Just as Tobias and Sarah did: by praying and living the "conjugal creed." A look at each of its components reveals the precise way for spouses of all times and places to *"prevent the evil spirit from having access to the soul"* so as *"to repel the evil* threatening to kill the body" (TOB 115:5). Only by entering ever more deeply into the mystery of the "conjugal creed" can we slowly, but surely, become the men and women we are created to be and, thereby, transform the culture of death into a culture of life.

The Bone Marrow of Their Conjugal Creed

In Genesis, the serpent wanted the first spouses to question God's benevolence, so he aimed his attack straight at God's character: "Did God *really* say ..." (see Gen 3:1). As a precise antidote to this attack on God's name, Tobias and Sarah begin their prayer with praise and thanksgiving: "Blessed are you, O God of our fathers, and blessed be your holy and glorious name forever. Let the heavens and the whole creation bless you" (Tobit 8:5).

In this way, John Paul says that Tobias and Sarah speak in some sense for all of creation — both visible and invisible. In the liturgy, the whole universe is taken up in an offering of praise to the Father. As the prophet Daniel demonstrates in his famous prayer, man's participation in the liturgy becomes the voice of all creation: "Bless the Lord, sun and moon ... stars of heaven ... rain and dew ... winter cold and summer heat ... mountains and hills ... all things that grow on the earth ... all birds of the air ... all beasts and cattle ... sing praise to him and highly exalt him forever" (Dan 3). "The cosmos is praying with us," says Pope Benedict. "It, too, is waiting for redemption" (SL, p. 70).

It is on this vast and "cosmic" background that both Tobias and Sarah recall with gratitude the creation of man as male and female (see TOB 116:1): "You made Adam and gave him Eve his wife as a helper and support. From them the race of mankind has sprung. You said, 'It is not good that the man should be alone; let us make a helper for him like himself'" (Tobit 8:6). The Pope infers that the truth expressed here — the truth of God's plan for man and woman "in the beginning"— is at the center of Tobias and Sarah's "religious consciousness." Indeed, it constitutes *the very bone marrow of their conjugal 'creed'"* (TOB 116:2).

By turning to these words of Genesis, the couple fully expresses the desire within their hearts. They long "to become a new link in the chain that goes back up to man's very beginnings." Precisely in this moment, before joining in conjugal union, "they commit themselves together to rereading the *'language of the body'* [according to] its divine source" (TOB 116:2). In this way, their conjugal creed becomes the specific antidote to the lust that the evil spirit wants to write into their hearts. If men and women of history are crippled by lust, Tobias and Sarah realize that "from the beginning it was not so" (Mt 19:8). Tobias and Sarah have *"rediscover[ed] the lost fullness of [their] humanity and want to regain it"* (TOB 43:7).

The Need for Full Purification

Tobias and Sarah "see with the eyes of faith the holiness of this vocation" (TOB 116:4). However, they are not granted an "automatic" purity. As fallen human beings, the new spouses sense their "need for a full purification," as the Pope puts it. Tobias expresses the purity of his intention: "And now, O Lord, I am not taking this sister of mine because of lust, but with sincerity." But he also knows that he is not able to carry out this intention without God's grace and mercy: "Grant that I may find mercy ... And Sarah said with him, 'Amen'" (Tobit 8:7–8).

Here we witness *"the moment of purification"* to which spouses must submit themselves if they wish, in becoming "one flesh," to express truthfully the sacramental sign of their covenant. Sexual intercourse must serve to build a true, loving communion between the spouses by expressing the sincere gift of oneself to the other (see TOB 116:3). This is impossible when spouses approach sexual intercourse merely as an outlet to indulge their lusts.

Tobias' words, "not because of lust," should be understood in the full context of all that John Paul teaches throughout his TOB about the "new ethos of redemption." Whereas the Christian "ethic" speaks of God's objective laws, Christian "ethos," as we learned earlier, refers to the subjective transformation of our hearts so that we come more and more to desire inwardly what God desires for us. Christ did not die on a cross and rise from the dead to give us a list of ethics to follow. He died on a cross and rose from the dead so that we, too, could live a new life (see Rom 6:4) – so that we could be free from sin, free from the domination of lustful impulses. As the *Catechism* teaches, "The Law of the Gospel ... does not add new external precepts, but proceeds to reform the heart" (CCC 1968). Through the ethos of redemption "the Spirit of the Lord gives new form to our desires, those inner movements that animate our lives" (CCC 2764).

Recall that "Christian ethos is characterized by *a transformation of the human person's conscience and attitudes ... such as to express and realize the value of the body and of sex* according to the Creator's original plan" (TOB 45:3). What hope! What joy! By God's grace we can truly reclaim the original truth of our sexuality and live it! Of course, none of this comes without a lively spiritual battle, as the story of Tobias and Sarah makes plain. But, as their story also makes plain, victory over lust *is* possible: "I am not taking this sister of mine because of lust, but with sincerity."

This kind of inner transformation marks the path to sanctity in marriage. And victory comes to the degree that we plunge ourselves into the "great mystery" of the liturgy. This, John Paul says, is the way in which the "language of the body" becomes the language of the liturgy: it must be "anchored in the deepest way possible, namely, by being set into the mystery of the 'beginning'" (TOB 116:2). For the "first man and the first woman must constitute ... the model of that communion for all men and women who in any period unite with each other so intimately that they are 'one flesh'" (TOB 10:3).

The Power of the Liturgy

Tobias and Sarah's prayer – their *"conjugal creed"* – "becomes in some way the deepest *model of the liturgy*" and a precise antidote to the diabolical scheming of the evil one. For liturgical prayer "is *a word of power*" drawn from the very sources of God's grace. This grace is precisely the power that frees us from evil and purifies us inwardly. In and through the power of the Church's liturgy, the sacrament of Marriage is brought into being. Spouses must draw from that power continually in their sacrament, so as to build their unity on the basis of a faithful reading of the language of their bodies (see TOB 115:6).

It is precisely the *power* of the liturgy that enables spouses to overcome the pull of lust in order to love each other "as Christ loved the Church" (Eph 5:25), in order to live and experience the ecstasy of the Song of Songs. Spouses "must implore [God] for such 'power' and for every other 'divine help' in prayer ... they must draw grace and love from the ever-living fountain of the Eucharist ... 'with humble perseverance' they must overcome their own faults and sins in the sacrament of Penance. These are the means – *infallible and indispensable* – to form the Christian spirituality of conjugal and familial life" (TOB 126:5). There is simply no other way to grow in true holiness than through a life of prayer and openness to God's grace and mercy poured out in the sacraments. "All of this is expressed in the language of the liturgy" (TOB 117b:2).

By taking up the "language of the liturgy," Tobias' love for Sarah
became a type, a foreshadowing, of Christ's love for the Church. Christ
stared death in the face on the "marriage bed" of the Cross, thus
consummating his love for the Church and conquering death by rising
to new life. Tobias also stared death in the face on his marriage bed,
and inspired with sacrificial (Christ-like) love, he also conquered death.
After seven men had succumbed, Tobias *consummates the marriage and lives!*
When God's design for marriage is your "conjugal creed," death has
no chance. Life refuses to surrender. Because of the eros-agape love
that united them in "one flesh," Tobias and Sarah witness to God as *the
God of life.* Their union joyously proclaims: "Where, O death, is your
victory? Where, O death, is your sting?" (I Cor 15:55).

But, one might ask, *What is the practical importance of all of this?* Why
did John Paul reflect on all of this, really? As I stated earlier, I do not
think a "symbolic" interpretation suffices. Without sensationalism,
without fanfare, but soberly and with great pastoral care, it seems John
Paul II wanted us to recognize that today — now, in *our* world, in *our*
relationships, in *our* marriages — there is an enemy attacking God's plan
for love and life and seeking to replace it with his diabolical plan of
lust and death. *And the only way out is to embrace this true "conjugal creed"* — to
open the union of man and woman to the grace and mercy to be found
only in the liturgy, that is, in man's *participation* in the saving death and
resurrection of Jesus Christ. Helping men and women to participate —
and participate *bodily* — in the saving death and resurrection of Christ:
that is what John Paul II's TOB is all about. And, as he himself said,
"Those who seek the fulfillment of their own human and Christian
vocation in marriage are called first of all to make ... this 'theology of
the body' ... the content of their lives and behavior" (TOB 23:5).

Dan and Kris' sad story demonstrates that "orthodoxy" in doctrine is not enough to make a marriage succeed. They both showed great enthusiasm for Church teaching. Dan, in fact, was pursuing a master's degree in theology with a focus on marriage and family studies. Kris was the leader of a Bible study group that met at her local parish. But Dan's theological knowledge and Kris's love of Scripture wasn't enough. What went wrong? In the language of John Paul II, Dan and Kris failed to sense their "need for a full purification." Dan and Kris needed a different kind of theological knowledge, the knowledge that is an interiorization of truth that takes ideas from the head to the heart.

The fallen dynamic of Adam and Eve goes very, very deep in us. Genesis expresses this dynamic when it says that the woman's desire (the Hebrew connotes a distorted desire) will be for her husband, and he will dominate her (see Gen 3:16). This was *not* God's original intention. This is the tragic result of sin. And theological knowledge alone cannot save us from the deep-rooted patterns of sin. Dan often used his theological knowledge, in fact, as a "fig leaf" to disguise a kind of intellectual domination over Kris.

Dan didn't consider himself the domineering type. He wasn't outwardly abusive or bossy. He wasn't *ever* going to slap his wife around or anything close to it. But "fallen Adam's" will to dominate asserted itself in Dan in other ways: he would often dismiss Kris's point of view and assert his own; he dominated conversation; he subtly criticized Kris for the way she dressed, the way she spoke, the music she listened to, and a host of other aspects of her personality that he didn't like; he would subtly manipulate her into sexual relations when it wasn't appropriate and sexual practices with which she was uncomfortable. And whenever Kris tried to speak up for herself, he would dominate that conversation too, effectively shutting her down.

"Fallen Eve" also went deep in Kris. Because she had such a strong "desire for her husband," she often gave in to Dan's domination for fear of rocking the boat and displeasing him. But the pain of being dominated would build up and then express itself in the subtle way she belittled Dan in front of others or mocked his masculinity. It was her revenge.

All hell broke loose in their relationship when Dan insisted that they engage in a certain form of foreplay to sexual intercourse that — while not objectively wrong — conjured up very painful memories for Kris because of a previous unhealthy relationship. Dan pressed the point and Kris, understandably, continued resisting. They both went to bed bitterly angry with each other. The next day Kris exploded: "You don't love me! You just want what you want! I'm so caught up in trying to please you and do everything you want me to do, I don't even know who I am anymore." Dan shot back: "Oh, and you claim to love me!? You can't stand me. Every time I risk sharing myself, you belittle me, emasculate me."

Full purification of that fallen dynamic of Adam and Eve is a painful, life-long journey. The shock of realizing how deep it goes in us – especially when we've convinced ourselves that we are further on the journey than we are – can be very difficult to recover from. Dan was willing to go to counseling. Kris wasn't and filed for divorce.

Reflection Questions

1. Dan and Kris' story show us that mere intellectual assent to Church teaching is not enough. In what ways might I still need to journey "from the head to the heart," allowing what I know to be true to bear fruit in my interior life?

2. If you are married (or hope to be married) can you imagine praying the "conjugal creed" before you unite with your spouse? What obstacles might exist to praying this prayer with your spouse? What practical steps can I take to overcome those obstacles?

Suggested Prayer

(Adapted from the prayer of Tobias and Sarah) Abba, you are my good, loving, generous Father. I want to enter into the song of all creation that continually rejoices in your goodness. For your goodness is revealed in all of creation, but especially in the creation of man as male and female and in their call to fruitful union. In the beginning, you made Adam and gave him Eve his wife as a helper and support. From their union, every generation, every human being, has sprung. You said that it's not good for the man to be alone, and so you planted deep within the human heart the desire for union with an "other."

But hidden in this erotic yearning for union is a divine secret, a doorway into a much greater mystery — a call to intimate union with *You* and the whole communion of saints. Grant me mercy for all the ways I have cheapened this "great mystery," and heal my heart to experience sexual love as it was meant to be. Amen.

Chapter 10

The Spousal Nature of the Liturgy

Angela is thirty-year-old single mom. Her son Jason is fifteen. After becoming familiar with John Paul II's TOB over the last two years, she is just now starting to look back at some of the painful events that have shaped and determined the course her life.

Angela was one of the first girls in her class to hit puberty. She already had full-sized breasts by fifth grade and with that came plenty of attention from the boys. At first, she liked the attention, even though it mostly consisted of boys goggling and snapping her bra strap. "I liked it, I think, because it filled a void," she says. "When I hit puberty, it was like I had contracted the plague or something, as far as my dad was concerned. He was always fairly distant from me and my younger sister. But it seemed once I had breasts, he wouldn't even come near me. I was starved for masculine affirmation. So I sought it in all the wrong ways. And I got it in all the wrong ways."

In both the Song of Songs and the marriage of Tobias and Sarah we see spouses rereading the language of the body in the truth. Both couples witness to the deepest meaning of the sacramental sign of marriage. They understand the truth of this sign not only in an *objective* sense. They also desire it *subjectively*. Their hearts *long* to express the full truth of their union as a sign of God's love and they recognize lust as a direct attack on that love. When this profound integration between objective reality (ethic) and subjective experience (ethos) occurs, John Paul says that spouses experience the language of the body for what it is. They experience it as *the language of the liturgy* (see TOB 116:5).

The normal context in which to enter the sacrament of Marriage is the sacrament of the Eucharist – the Mass. Here we see vividly, right in the liturgical ritual itself, the link that Ephesians 5 draws between the union of spouses and the union of Christ and the Church – "'For this reason a man shall leave his father and mother and be joined to his wife, and the two shall become one flesh.' This is a great mystery, and I mean in reference to Christ and the church" (Eph 5:31-32). By the very fact that Marriage takes place in the context of the Eucharist, we see how the liturgy itself brings "these two signs together [marital union and Eucharist], making of them *the single great sign*, that is, *a great sacrament*" (TOB 95b:7). As we said earlier, this means not only that spousal love and union are modeled after the liturgy, but *the Church's whole liturgical ritual is modeled after spousal love and union* (see TOB 117:6).

When the Language of the Liturgy Becomes the "Language of the Body"

"Already baptism ... is a nuptial mystery" (CCC 1617). At the Easter Vigil, when the Christ candle is plunged into the baptismal font "in the name of the Father, and of the Son, and the Holy Spirit," it symbolizes, among other things, the Heavenly Bridegroom impregnating the womb of the Church from which many children will be born again – not of a husband's seed, but born of God (see Jn

I:13). Reflecting on the "scandal" of this symbolism, Catholic author Christopher Derrick wrote:

> There are a number of respects in which the Church can be a good deal more shocking than some forms of Catholic piety would wish it to be ... The Catholic Faith is an incarnational, even carnal thing: I have heard it described as the sexiest of all the world's religions. The uniting of flesh and blood with the supremely Sacred lies at the heart of its belief and its worship too, and a bodily and even sexual emphasis recurs constantly in its self-expression. A Catholic cannot recite his Creeds without mentioning begetting, conception, and birth: he cannot say the Hail Mary without mentioning the female generative tract, or the *Te Deum* without praising the Lord for finding nothing there of the indecent ... nothing to abhor. He sees the whole relationship between God and man in quasi-sexual, quasi-generative terms. (SSV, pp. 72-73)

"Quasi" is, of course, an important qualifier. God is not sexual (see CCC 42, 239, 370). But, based on a certain similarity – while always maintaining the greater dissimilarity – sexual imagery, as we have been learning throughout this book, provides a glimmer, a hint, a clue into the divine secret, a way of entering into "heaven's song." The source and summit of all this quasi-sexual imagery is, of course, the Eucharist. In the Eucharist, Christ and his Bride enter sacramentally into their spousal union consummated at the Cross. Bishop Fulton

Sheen brilliantly illuminates the spousal nature of the Lord's sacrifice as follows:

> Now we've always thought, and rightly so, of Christ the Son on the Cross and the mother beneath him. But that's not the complete picture. That's not the deep understanding. Who is our Lord on the Cross? He's the new Adam. Where's the new Eve? At the foot of the Cross. ... How did the old humanity begin? With the nuptials. How will the new humanity begin? With the nuptials. If Eve became the mother of the living in the natural order, is not this woman at the foot of the Cross to become another mother? And so the bridegroom looks down at the bride. He looks at his beloved. Christ looks at his Church. There is here the birth of the Church. As St. Augustine puts it, and here I am quoting him verbatim, "The heavenly bridegroom left the heavenly chambers, with the presage of the nuptials before him. He came to the marriage bed of the Cross, a bed not of pleasure, but of pain, united himself with the woman, and consummated the union forever. As it were, the blood and water that came from the side of Christ was the spiritual seminal fluid." And so from these nuptials "Woman, there's your son" this is the beginning of the Church. (FS, p. 60)

I would like to elaborate on this line in particular: "How did the old humanity begin? With the nuptials. How will the new humanity begin? With the nuptials." We are all born of the physical, mortal seed given by fallen Adam to fallen Eve. And we must all be "born again" (Jn 3:3) of the invisible, immortal seed (see 1 Pt 1:23) given by the New Adam to the New Eve. Nuptials! *Nuptials lie at the heart and center, source and summit of our Christian faith.* The mystery of sexual difference and the two becoming "one flesh," in fact, undergirds the whole economy of God's revelation. Recall, as John Paul II asserts, that the visible sign of marriage is *"the foundation of the whole sacramental order"* (TOB 95b:7). Right from the beginning, the joining of the two in "one flesh" points us to the summit of God's eternal plan for man and for the universe that all things in heaven and on earth might be "one" in fruitful union with Jesus Christ (see Eph 1:10). This is what is enacted and accomplished by the Church's liturgy: God's holy nuptials! – his espousing of his own creation.

This is the deepest essence and meaning of human embodiment, of sexual desire, and of erotic love. They are meant to enable us to "enter into" heaven's song. Perhaps now we can better understand why, of all the books in the Bible, the Song of Songs is in the center. Perhaps now we can better understand why the Song of Songs is the "authentic soundtrack" of Christianity. And perhaps now we can better sense the "weight" of Tobias and Sarah's grave situation and, even more so, the *power* of their prayer, their "conjugal creed," their liturgical proclamation. It enabled them to rediscover sexual love *as it was meant to be* and, through that, to enter into deep intimacy with God.

No less is at stake today when the two become "one flesh." Our choices and our actions in this regard always "take on the whole weight of human existence" (TOB 115:3). Whom will we serve? What spirit will we allow to have sway in us? The *evil spirit* that writes lust and death into our hearts, or the *Holy Spirit* who writes love and life?

Studying John Paul's teaching about lust has helped Angela to understand her father's treatment of her. She recalls as a girl discovering a closet full of pornographic magazines in his office. "That probably explains why he was scared to death of me when I started developing. He was a lust-aholic. He was always saying crude things about women. This has been very painful to come to terms with, but I think he resented me because my body stirred his lusts. He couldn't deal with the internal contradiction of lusting after his own daughter, so he just didn't want to be around me. I don't think he's ever hugged me since I hit puberty. He barely looks me in the eye. My dad even hinted about the possibility of an abortion when I got pregnant. It all just makes me sick."

Angela is now engaged to Gary – who, in fact, was the one who introduced her to John Paul II's TOB. "His love has really enabled me to look at these painful things in my life. I know Gary really wants to marry me, but he keeps telling me that Jesus is my true Bridegroom. Coming to see that Jesus loves my body and created my body to reveal his own love – oh my gosh, that's just amazing! It's so healing. Gary and I really want to live this. We really want to open our union to God and let it glorify him. And we want to help many other people live it as well."

Gary legally adopted Jason as his son when he and Angela married. They are both studying to be counselors with the goal of bringing the teaching of John Paul II into their practice.

Reflection Questions

1. Have I ever previously considered that the Church's liturgy is modeled after the love of spouses? We spoke above of this "spousal imprint" in baptism and the Eucharist. Where do we see this spousal reality in the other sacraments?

2. What bearing might the spousal mystery have on the fact that only a man can receive the sacrament of Holy Orders?

3. Are there hidden shames or fears in my heart that need to be addressed in order to embrace and rejoice in the spousal and erotic symbolism of the Church's liturgical life? Do I believe that Christ can heal those wounds and cast out those fears? Do I want him to?

Suggested Prayer

Come Holy Spirit, come! Fill our hearts, our minds, our bodies! Enkindle in us the fire of your blazing love. Overshadow the Church, just as you did Mary, so that Christ might be eternally conceived in her. Renew her in her celebration of the liturgy. Help all members of the body of Christ to see and enter into the spousal mystery of the sacraments. Come Holy Spirit, come into the hearts of spouses everywhere, inspiring them to open to you whenever they become one-flesh, and through this divinely inspired *eros*, renew the face of the earth. Amen.

Epilogue:

Where Do I Go from Here?

You have just finished reading a challenging book. John Paul II's Theology of the Body is mystical stuff, and mystical theology is never something easily grasped. It needs time to penetrate. So where do you go from here? Actually, the first thing I would recommend is to read this book again. But this time, take it with you into the adoration chapel. That, in fact, as I learned during a visit with Cardinal Dziwisz, is where John Paul II wrote his TOB, before the tabernacle in his private chapel. So, I would suggest not merely that you read through this book again: *pray through it* with expectant faith that Christ desires to pour out his healing and integrating love into those wounded places of our hearts. If you found anything in this book particularly difficult or even troubling, take those things into prayer. Test everything, probe everything, submit everything in prayer to Christ. I am a fallible author and a fallible interpreter of John Paul II's work, but I am confident that Christ will show you what, if anything, in this book he desires for you to spend more time with.

The second thing I would recommend is for you to place what you have learned in this book in the context of John Paul II's entire TOB. If you have the aptitude, I would strongly encourage you to study John Paul's entire text directly (make sure you have the Waldstein translation). If you find that difficult – truth be told, even many seasoned theologians do – you could start with my commentary

Theology of the Body Explained or my short overview *Theology of the Body for Beginners*. You may also be interested in attending one of the five-day intensive courses I teach through the Theology of the Body Institute (www.tobinstitute.org). There are also many other fine teachers and writers on the TOB to whose wisdom you should expose yourself, especially if you have already studied my materials. Each brings his or her own unique perspective and emphases which will certainly enrich your overall understanding. Just do a search for "theology of the body" online to discover some of these other fine authors.

Finally, I would recommend a little booklet by St. Louis de Montfort entitled *The Secret of Mary*. An Internet search will lead you to it (I prefer the version adapted by Eddie Doherty for Montfort Publications). This provides a very good, brief summary of his much longer treatise *True Devotion to the Blessed Virgin*. I have grown more and more convinced that de Montfort's formula for devotion to Mary is critical in coming to understand and live the mystical wisdom of John Paul II's TOB. I have one caveat, however, regarding de Montfort's writings. I am in agreement with those who find some of his language and comparisons troubling. As the Introduction to the Montfort Publications edition of *True Devotion* states, "His theological outlook and his style of writing may not suit everyone: he wrote some 250 years ago. A work written in an age and environment so different from our own will necessarily sound strange to modern ears. Certain expressions and comparisons may tend to put us off." John Paul II, himself, observed that de Montfort's writing "can be a bit disconcerting, given its rather florid and baroque style." That said, "the essential theological truths which it contains are undeniable" (GM, p. 29).

Personally, as I have prayerfully "entered into" the theological truths set forth by de Montfort (it has taken me several readings over many years to discover the real treasure below the surface), a gateway to deep communion with Christ has opened up. Mary *is* that gateway. As we entrust ourselves entirely to her motherly, loving care, Mary, the woman of the Song of Songs, will teach us how to open to the Beloved as she does — with total, trusting abandonment. And she will teach us how to sing the Song …

Index

About the Author

C hristopher West is recognized around the world for his work promoting an integral vision of human life, love, and sexuality. He serves as a research fellow and faculty member of the Theology of the Body Institute near Philadelphia. He has also lectured on a number of other prestigious faculties, offering graduate and undergraduate courses at St John Vianney Seminary in Denver, the John Paul II Institute in Melbourne, Australia, and the Institute for Priestly Formation at Creighton University in Omaha.

In addition, Christopher is the best-selling author of several books and one of the most sought-after speakers in the Church today, having delivered more than 1,000 public lectures on four continents, in a dozen countries, and in more than 200 American cities. His popular column "Body Language" is syndicated to diocesan newspapers around the country. Christopher and his wife, Wendy, live with their five children near Lancaster, Pennsylvania.